PRAISE FOR *WE REFUSE TO FORGET*

"Black Creek stories, rich with both the subtleties and the crudenesses of America's racial history, force us all to contemplate new forms of reckoning." —*The New Yorker*

"An illuminating look at racial dynamics within [the] Creek Nation . . . Sharp character sketches, incisive history lessons, and Gayle's autobiographical reflections as a Jamaican American transplant to Oklahoma make this a powerful portrait of how white supremacy 'divides marginalized groups and pits them against each other.'"

—*Publishers Weekly* (starred review)

"Caleb Gayle's rich and important book reminds us that American history is more surprising, terrible, and, yes, inspiring than we often care to know. The history he weaves is deeply relevant to today's movements for racial justice and Indigenous rights, as well as to the enduring and quintessential question 'Who is an American?' I'm grateful for the painstaking work Gayle has done to answer this question for all of us."

—Heather McGhee, author of *The Sum of Us*

"Caleb Gayle—as a journalist, the son of Jamaican immigrants, and a son of the country—has written a gripping history of the fully Black and fully Creek citizens of the tribe who have struggled against both the Republic and the Creek Nation to secure their rightful place in both. He tells a complicated story of the past and in doing so sheds light on the ways our fantasies of race endure and are, gradually, being undone. A vital work." —David Treuer, author of *The Heartbeat of Wounded Knee*

"When Caleb Gayle wrote this book, he reached back into history to find power. By telling the stories of elders like Cow Tom and other Black Creeks who refused to simplify our understanding of race, he amplified that our stories escape categories because our lives are rich and complex. In the end, he let us not forget that America can handle every part that makes us whole."

—Ibram X. Kendi, National Book Award–winning author of
Stamped from the Beginning and *How to Be an Antiracist*

"*We Refuse to Forget* reminds readers, on damn near every page, that we are collectively experiencing a brilliance we've seldom seen or imagined. Caleb Gayle welcomes us and then deftly interrogates and really initiates the parts of my experience and imagination that I do not want to wholly accept as home. *We Refuse to Forget* is a new standard in book-making."

—Kiese Laymon, author of the bestselling *Heavy: An American Memoir*

"Caleb Gayle is both historian and griot. *We Refuse to Forget* is an important part of American history told with a clear-eyed and forceful brilliance."

—Jacqueline Woodson, National Book Award–winning
author of *Red at the Bone*

"A good reminder of a forgotten piece of American history about the Creek Nation, which both enslaved Blacks and accepted Blacks as citizens."   —*The Atlanta Journal-Constitution*

WE REFUSE TO FORGET

A TRUE STORY OF
BLACK CREEKS,
AMERICAN IDENTITY,
AND POWER

CALEB GAYLE

RIVERHEAD BOOKS

NEW YORK

RIVERHEAD BOOKS
An imprint of Penguin Random House LLC
penguinrandomhouse.com

The Library of Congress has catalogued the Riverhead hardcover edition as follows:

Names: Gayle, Caleb, author.
Title: We refuse to forget : a true story of Black Creeks,
American identity, and power / Caleb Gayle.
Description: New York : Riverhead Books, 2022. |
Includes index.
Identifiers: LCCN 2021053867 (print) | LCCN 2021053868 (ebook) |
ISBN 9780593329580 (hardcover) | ISBN 9780593329597 (ebook)
Subjects: LCSH: Creek Indians—Mixed descent. | Creek Indians—
Tribal citizenship. | Creek Indians—Ethnic identity. | Blacks—
Relations with Indians. | Muscogee (Creek) Nation—History.
Classification: LCC E99.C9 G36 2022 (print) | LCC E99.C9 (ebook) |
DDC 975.004/97385—dc23/eng/20211105
LC record available at https://lccn.loc.gov/2021053867
LC ebook record available at https://lccn.loc.gov/2021053868

First Riverhead hardcover edition: June 2022
First Riverhead trade paperback edition: June 2023
Riverhead trade paperback ISBN: 9780593329603

Printed in the United States of America
1 3 5 7 9 10 8 6 4 2

BOOK DESIGN BY MEIGHAN CAVANAUGH

For Peanut,
for the fam, and
for those whose stories
are yet to be told

CONTENTS

PART II

WHO WE CAN BECOME

"I GOT INDIAN IN ME"

It seemed that to capture the multiplicity and contradictory nature of this past, I would have to tell at least two stories— sketch two histories, enter two worlds, enlist two purposes, and sound two calls for justice—at once.

DR. TIYA MILES

My Jamaican family moved from New York City to Tulsa, Oklahoma, in the late 1990s with few expectations of running into a Black person. In a place that at the time was far less Black than the New York we had left, we were desperate to find people whose skin resembled ours in the institutions that could make us feel at home. Soon after moving, my parents found a Black church in North Tulsa, the part of the city where most of the Black people live and the place where seventy years earlier Black Wall Street once stood tall and sprawled wide.

When I was a kid there, most of these Black folks, especially those who had some history in this buckle of the Bible Belt, were known to say a peculiar, indelicate phrase that now sounds so familiar: "I got Indian in me." Their ancestors likely included people who had called one of the Five Nations home. I didn't know it then, but the Five Nations were actually called Five Civilized Tribes, an even more indelicate way of designating the Cherokee, Choctaw, Chickasaw, Creek, and Seminole Indians in Oklahoma since at least 1866. But the kids who'd say that likely did not know this history, and neither did I. They passed as simply Black. At least I thought they did.

As a child, I thought that Black people in America came from only a few places. From Africa, and recently. From a Caribbean country (like my parents), also recently. Or—by way of slave ships—from the African continent hundreds of years ago. I assumed the kids who said "I got Indian in me" were spreading myths or trying to explain why their skin was somewhat lighter and their hair a bit curlier than mine.

But I dismissed these ideas too early. Those kids didn't know the historical power they wielded in that phrase because what they were saying was a simple sentence born of a strange, forgotten history, one hard to imagine in the bright bustle of turn-of-the-millennium America. Even in the second decade of the twenty-first century—as Oklahoma fights over land, as courthouses hear challenges over identity, and as jurisdiction over these lands, Muscogee Creek Nation lands, has become a matter of Supreme Court cases such as *McGirt v. Oklahoma*—it is hard to grasp.

But it is true.

What my young friends didn't know when they boasted about their DNA was that their Native and Black ancestors walked hundreds of miles together from the southeastern United States to reach what became Oklahoma. Nor did they know that some of these Black ancestors came as slaves, others as adopted citizens, and still others as fully recognized members of the Creek Nation.

And I'm willing to bet that none of them ever heard the name of one Black man, a former putative slave who walked the Trail of Tears, a man dubbed "Cow Tom" by his former owner, a Creek chief. Like countless Native Americans, Cow Tom made that long, dangerous trek before he ultimately rose to leadership within the Creek Nation. In fact, it was Cow Tom who kept my friends' Creek identity intact when he negotiated an 1866 treaty with the U.S. government, an agreement that included citizenship rights for all Black people within the Creek Nation—whether slave, adopted, or free.

It may seem odd that a son of Jamaican parents would find his way inside American history, especially inside the history of Black people about whom you've likely never heard in a state you've likely never visited.

Like all history, how it started wasn't how anyone expected it to end.

One day in 2018, I was sitting in the New York office of the British newspaper *The Guardian*. I had worked there as a writer for four or five months. On this day, I was jostling between empty rooms and unoccupied desks while more senior writers and editors went to meetings, lunches, and vacations.

I had no story on the books, and my editor and I had a meeting soon to figure out what I'd write next. I sat at my computer and typed "www.tulsaworld.com" into my web browser, not because I was looking for inspiration but because I wanted a reminder that people could cover news and write stories about places and people most of the world didn't care about. What came up across the top of the *Tulsa World*'s home page were familiar faces and a story that claimed that the Black people in the accompanying picture had been members of a Nation that wasn't the United States and had freedom that their ancestors had given them in the Creek Nation but not in the United States.

I was intrigued and called some friends I grew up with, many of whom had told me when we were kids that they were part Indian. I knew I had a story, but I didn't realize that the piece I'd eventually write for *The Guardian* would lead me on a journey that reconfigured my notions of identity, race, and belonging.

Looking back, it is odd that I wrote a story about Oklahoma, a place I wanted to forget and a state whose mere mention often prompted any friend from anywhere else to ask, "Where is Oklahoma again?" In telling you about the place that became my home, I can tell you about America and how America fashions its identity. And if this story has shown me anything, it's that there is nothing simple about who you are or where you come from. Like the people on the front page of the *Tulsa World*—descendants of Cow Tom and other former Black citizens of the Creek Nation—we are all beautifully complex, and there's nothing more American than struggling to fit all that complexity into boxes you did not create in the first place.

WE OFTEN FORGET who we are because we have never been given the chance to remember properly. The anti-lynching memorial at the National Memorial for Peace and Justice in Montgomery, Alabama, offers a radical chance to remember not just the highlights of the civil rights movement but also the true pain and brutality of our nation's past. Such painful remembering of the violence that white people perpetrated against Black people is required before we can build true racial reconciliation. Remembering with eyes wide open, I believe, is the first step to living out our moral obligations today.

The fact that my classmates and I in Tulsa in the late twentieth century didn't understand where we came from wasn't just bad schooling. It was the result of a deliberate attempt to prevent us from remembering. Which is another way of saying that from an early age, Black people were stopped from working to change a world that had been built on racialized, violent foundations.

But what if we did know? What if we all knew about this story?

Knowing this history would make the truth clearer. We'd know, for example, how Tulsa's struggles over land use, development, and zoning mask a larger story, one where city planners deliberately designed the city to ensure that different nonwhite populations would compete with one another instead of banding together to push back against the white ruling class.

We'd know that the Cherokee people have as much right to seat a representative in Congress as do Puerto Rico and the District of Columbia. And they have this right based on signed treaties with the U.S. government, which the government has chosen to ignore.

We'd know that the Black members of the Creek Nation who were ejected from the tribe in 1979 should be reinstated into their political homeland. Nothing should be allowed to nullify the cultural promise and legal compact between the founding Nation and its new members, no matter their race or background.

And we'd know, once and for all, that white power and white supremacy are as old as the nation itself, as dangerous today as they were centuries ago. The history of Cow Tom's people demonstrates that white identity is too often used as a tool to divide those who are deemed "other," "irrelevant," or "dangerous."

And we'd know that white supremacy's true goal is to violently disrupt lives where there is money to be made and to erase from our collective cultural and political memories any path to becoming American that white men didn't create.

At the same time, knowing this history also makes some ideas less clear. For example, it's an open question just how the descendants of "Creek Freedmen" identify today. Some see themselves as Black, others as Indigenous, others as both, and others as simply American because they—like most of us—just don't know whence they came.

How should the country at large see these people? What duties does the government have to such an aggrieved, narrowly defined group of people? Do these labels matter? And perhaps the broadest question of all: What is the past and the future of identity in America?

For himself and his family, Cow Tom secured land, built a home, and grew wealthy. He left his family the guarantee of full citizenship in the Creek Nation even when the U.S. government did not provide Blacks the same courtesy. He left for his descendants bread crumbs to guide them on their journey to define their identity, tools to advocate for the citizenship he helped to secure.

Cow Tom founded a home for Black people in the Creek Nation. Like so many of the founders of United States, what he left us is more than just words on a constitution or platitudinous statements of values in treaties, ancestors with a famous pedigree, or artifacts from his life. He left the Creek Nation a chance to be better and his people a way to be freer. He left all of us an incredible story that once we learn it, we must then refuse to forget. We must hold fast—like this family has held fast—to the stories that make us who we are.

WHICH BRINGS ME back to the article in the *Tulsa World*, which was an account of a lawsuit in Oklahoma that captured my attention.

On one side are the plaintiffs: people who say, as their ancestors have said for more than a century, that they're both fully Black and fully Creek. They are represented by attorney Damario Solomon-Simmons, who is himself directly descended from Cow Tom.

On the other side is the defendant: the Creek Nation, which in 1866 signed a treaty with the U.S. government that gave certain Black people citizenship rights in the Nation. Decades later, in 1979, in a prolonged yet stunning about-face, the Creek Nation took away those rights to citizenship with the approval and support of the U.S. government.

The plaintiffs want to be reenfranchised, and it isn't the first time they've made such a request. And regardless of the number of times they've lodged this legal claim, they resiliently remind the courts that they want to return to and be treated as equals within the political community that is the Creek Nation. The defendant seeks to keep these people out: Creek leaders do not want anyone but the people they believe are Indigenous enough to be considered citizens. And Black Creek folks are too Black to be Creek enough to have the citizenship their ancestors had.

Some observers say that the Creek wish to preserve their political autonomy in the face of external meddling; others, that the Nation embraces a concept that sits uncomfortably in the United States of today: the granting or rescinding of citizenship merely because of race.

The story is as odd as it sounds: one marginalized group taking another marginalized Nation to court for what to outsiders might feel like hollow ends. But the descendants of Cow Tom and the descendants of other Black Creeks aren't suing just for citizenship. They're reclaiming their families' stake in the country's journey. Who they are, they know, is both fully Black and fully Creek. Citizenship in the Creek Nation gave Cow Tom's descendants land—and, consequently, wealth, status, power, and opportunity—at a time when the U.S. government wasn't ready to give Blacks the same opportunities.

For Damario Solomon-Simmons's ancestors, being Black didn't mean what being Black meant to others in mid-nineteenth-century America. Each of his lawsuits against the Creek Nation acknowledges the violence and disenfranchisement that crushed the lives of thousands and illuminates the overlooked, inspiring, and original ways that marginalized people pushed back, worked together, and redefined their world.

Perhaps remembering a different story of Blackness can uncover new paths forward for Blackness and other marginalized identities. Perhaps refusing to forget this—a story that is uniquely American— we might carve expansive ways to also be and feel American. Because this story is as strange and terrible as it is empowering: how a collection of exiles violently excluded by a U.S. government intent on spreading white supremacy found a way to band together, forge new alliances, and build a new identity on the wreckage of what they'd had before.

Today, how we decide who is or is not American is again a pressing question. Another is understanding how white supremacy divides marginalized groups and pits them against each other, to the detriment of all. What has been at stake in this case is the chance to cement who the plaintiffs are by telling the court who they and their ancestors have been. And in their doing so, their sheer persistence to tell their own stories should signal to any person who has been marginalized, any person who has been judged for their appearance, or any person who has been denied their history that they and their stories *belong*.

This family story is also the story of the Black Creeks. It is the story of how America remembers itself, how it mourns, how it grows up. Damario Solomon-Simmons's story, just like that of his ancestor Cow Tom, is alive and well. It is the story of you and of me.

PART I

WHO WE'VE BEEN

CHAPTER 1

COLLATERAL DAMAGE

He was compelled to seek safety by hasty flight.

COW TOM, LOYAL CREEK
ABSTRACT #160, 1870

For weeks, the battle had been raging not far from Cow Tom's home. Smoke from artillery fire hung in the air, and the groans of injured and dying men were constant day and night. This Civil War battle happened outside the United States, and it disrupted the lives of people the United States had turned from native dwellers to foreigners.

ON JULY 15, 1863, Major General James Blunt of the Union Army called on his 250 cavalry soldiers to bring with them their guns, swords, and four pieces of heavy artillery. Familiar sights and sounds of battle preparation animated the day: the galloping of horses, the continual barking of orders at all hours of the night, cleaning of weaponry and equipment to pass the time waiting for a battle they knew would come even if they didn't know when. Young men had received orders from Blunt to walk along the eastern bulge of the Arkansas River in Indian Territory as they awaited to know their fates—clarity that the general just couldn't give them.

OVER THE NEXT TWO DAYS, Blunt guided his troops through the last thirteen miles of thicket, forest, wood, and river. For a brief two hours, his men—eventually a little less than three thousand in total—sat just over a mile from the Confederate enemy, who had been resting. Blunt's soldiers grabbed water from a nearby ridge to slake their thirst and unpacked their haversacks, whose contents included notes from home, Bibles, and most important, food kept safe by the sacks' stitching and weaving reinforced by tar.

BY TEN A.M. ON JULY 17, the men of the Union Army were assembled into two columns. According to Blunt, "The infantry was in column by companies, the cavalry by platoons and artillery by sections, and all closed in mass so as to deceive the enemy in regard to the strength of my force. In this order I moved up rapidly to within one-fourth of a mile of [the Confederate] line, when both columns were suddenly deployed to the right and left, and in less than five minutes my whole force was in line of battle, covering the enemy's entire front."

The Confederates were under the command of General Douglas H. Cooper, who had been dispatched to defend what had become a major supply route. His Confederate comrades had arrived in this part of Indian Territory not more than a year before and in short order had put up a commissary, a field hospital, arbors, and housing tents. Built along the Canadian River, the settlement had ample fresh water for both the troops and, just as important, the livestock.

But this wasn't just an ideal place to set up a field hospital and house troops. The twenty-five miles from where General Blunt started his advance on this group of Confederate soldiers was in a town called Honey Springs, in a part of the continent that had not yet been determined to be part of either the United States or the Confederacy. This was Indian Territory. Honey Springs was along the main route that connected the outer lands that were disputed by the Union and the Confederacy, an area that included Texas, Kansas, Missouri, and Arkansas. Honey Springs was a stagecoach stop, a watering hole, and a weigh and refueling station. Along this trail Confederate soldiers received and distributed provisions, weapons, timber, and livestock. But as the Civil War raged, this area became even more critical as the Union wanted to fight proxy battles on native land.

But the land on which these soldiers fought—where men Black, white, and Indigenous died—was not in America. The Civil War wasn't just fought on American soil. One hundred seven such Civil War battles were fought outside America—fought in the metaphorical backyards of Native people. The Battle of Honey Springs took place just steps from Cow Tom, whose later actions prompted generations to tell others, "I got Indian in me."

The Union defeated the Confederates at Honey Springs, and in the battle's aftermath Cooper's army looked to decamp until they determined where to go next. They came across empty homes and farms in the area in which food and water had been left by people fleeing the fighting across the region. The battles had hollowed out towns like Coosa, Coweta, Tuckabatchee, North Fork, Canadian Colored, and Arkansas Colored. Creek towns. And the land on which the Confederates fought was Creek land, belonging to the citizens of the Creek Nation.

A nation once unified was scattered. Homes left in the state of people set to flee at moment's notice, farms and cattle left unattended, ways of life abandoned. Scores of Creek families headed north to Kansas with whatever they could pack, trying to escape the war they didn't ask for.

By August 1863, Confederate soldiers made their way twelve miles from North Fork, where they lost their way along the Canadian River and discovered that not all Creek territory had been abandoned. They came upon a curious group of Creek families who had stayed—and who looked like the people whom neither the U.S. Constitution nor the Constitution of the Confederate States recognized fully as people.

One of those people was Cow Tom. He had stayed, and so had a host of other refugee Creeks, some of whom shared his jet-black skin tone and some of whom didn't. When these Confederate soldiers—tired, hungry, desperate, and likely not appreciative of the Black Creek cause—descended on Cow Tom's land and the land of his neighbors, it became clear that the Creeks' presence on their land wasn't greeted with enthusiasm by the Confederates.

DAYS INTO THE EVER-GROWING PRESENCE of Confederate soldiers on his land, Cow Tom and his wife, Amy, took what they could pack onto their backs and left. They walked away from everything that they had known—where they had raised a son, where they had run a grist mill, where they'd farmed and raised cattle—and plunged into a dark unknown. Night was the only time they could travel because that was the only time they could move undetected. With Confederate rebels in the area doing whatever overzealous white colonists might do—claiming for themselves land and property that was someone else's—they didn't know what they'd encounter. There was no guarantee that any people they met would be friendly, particularly if those people were hungry and war-worn Confederate rebels. There was very little chance that Cow Tom would be seen as what he was: fully Creek and fully Black, and free. It was virtually certain that any white person they'd encounter would see Cow Tom as just a slave running from his master.

His days would never dull the hopes for the grist mill he once told a U.S. official he badly wanted or his dream of a school for his children and grandchildren to attend.

After more than a week of being on the run, Cow Tom and his band of travelers—hungry, wet from continuous rain, having suffered cold nights and been burned by the daytime sun, and insufficiently nourished—came to what seemed like a place to rest. They made it to an outpost called Fort Gibson with no certainty that they'd be accepted. There was no guarantee that Fort Gibson still sat under the control of the side that was supposedly against slavery. But it didn't matter: Cow Tom "was compelled to seek safety by hasty flight," he said later, because the skirmish between warring white people had laid waste to all he knew. And since he wasn't alone and a brazen, pioneering brand of leadership seemed core to his existence, he had to lead a Nation that like so many other marginalized peoples in America had become collateral damage to the U.S. government's ambitions.

CHAPTER 2

ENOUGH FAMILY.
LET'S CREATE A NATION

The white people intend to take all their lands.

UNNAMED CREEK HEADMAN, MAY 2, 1763

Most American schoolchildren who have taken a basic history course can tell you that the United States experienced its fair share of battles before most say it was founded in 1776. As a student, I was fascinated by the stories of Pontiac, the Ottawa chief during the French and Indian War. I read as much as I could about the British, French, and American soldiers duking it out over what they saw as unsettled land, battling over who would rule this "new" nation. I followed the stories of Spanish conquistadores owning Florida, losing Florida, and gaining Florida again only to ultimately lose it.

What this instruction didn't explore was the lives of those people who lived, cultivated, and cared for this land first. When the Europeans came to North America, Indigenous groups were forced to decide how to deal with them, employing in turn the tools of diplomacy and the weapons of war to survive. As these invading white men took their land, Indigenous people watched, fought, and prayed, as the old hymn put it, over how much of their land would be taken over. And when they inevitably were faced with deciding whom to side with and whom to oppose, these Native tribes and Nations faced critical decisions that would determine survival or certain death.

Creeks especially had to practice a special brand of diplomacy. From 1754 to 1763, the British colonies in North America fought against New France's colonies, and both Britain and France had the help of Indigenous allies. The French seemingly needed these Indigenous peoples more than the British because the British already had nearly two million people living in their colonies, many of whom they could conscript into battle, while the French had only about sixty thousand. To counteract the British superiority in numbers, the French enlisted the efforts of their "allies" in the Wabanaki Confederacy, which contained numerous tribes, while the British had the Iroquois, the Catawba, and the Cherokee fighting for them.

The British ultimately prevailed in the French and Indian War, though each side gave up land they owned—because white men get to say what they own even if they only owned it because they proclaimed it so. For the Creek, victory for the British Crown spelled an end to its preferred posture: neutrality. And the end of neutrality meant that its future would be uncertain.

Before the war, the Creek maintained their neutrality, as historian Steven Hahn put it, "to defend Creek territory from unwanted intrusion of backcountry settlers," and to sit apart from those Nations that pinned their hopes on one imperial colonial power triumphing over the other. Long before the extreme bloodshed of the nine-year war, the Creeks made clear their neutrality: in 1713, the Creeks signed what became known as the Coweta Resolution, which established their position of neutrality among Great Britain, France, and Spain. It was a uniting banner under which the Creeks became known to European colonists: standing aloof in this evolving, rapidly changing landscape.

With Britain victorious in the French and Indian War, all of this changed. War no longer distracted the British Crown from subordinating its colonies in North America and all who lived there, Creeks included. The Creeks long feared what would happen if one country emerged on top in this bloody war, which had taken the lives of more than ten thousand by disease, more than fifteen hundred by wounds, and roughly the same number killed in action. The Creeks knew then, as many learned later, that whoever won would fix their eyes on Creek land as well as the fertile lands of other Indigenous people.

The Creeks saw it coming.

Even during the war, the British compelled the Creeks to cede parts of their territory in Georgia to the British Crown—territory that the Creeks had called their own for centuries. So when the war ended, they knew what was coming. The ending of this war would start, in historian Angie Debo's unsettling phrase, a long "road to disappearance" for the people who had known America long before America was America.

. . .

MOST NATIONS are founded by conquest. But the British, the French, and the Spanish founded their North American colonies, first, on the power of their words: "It is now ours." By contrast, the Creek Nation was invented by survival.

Long before the British, the French, and the Spanish arrived on American shores, the predecessors to what we now call the Creek Nation formed bonds based on communal understandings of land shared one with another. But this survival enriched everyone: tribe after tribe, all bound by the realization that they all were to share the land.

The Creeks were scaffolded by bonds—deep bonds. It took until the end of the Civil War for the Creek Nation to build itself into what we know it to be today, replete with a constitution that the United States recognizes, with three branches of government. But the mechanics of a government existed long before the United States asked this confederacy of kinship to become a Nation.

The Creek lands—now primarily southern Tennessee, all of Alabama, western Georgia, and part of northern Florida, though a smattering of settlements could be found even more expansively—were outlined by small townships often founded by families and clans that established relationships with other families and clans, often through marriage. These towns were run by councils chaired by a leader or chief called a mico (spelled also "micco" or "mikko").

Long before the British began laying claim to the Nation, kinship, family, and loyalty knit together this sprawling confederation of tribes they called "Creek."

It is often in nostalgia—the dreaming and wishing for another moment of "yesterday"—that we learn most about who we were and who we could be. Pleasant Porter, a Creek chief, did a lot of dreaming. In Porter's annual address to the Creek Nation Council, he concluded with a bold remark. "The vitality of our race still persists. We have not lived for naught. We are the original discoverers of this continent and the conquerors of it from the animal kingdom and from it first taught the art of peace and war, and first planted the institutions of virtue, truth, and liberty." No stranger to reminding white colonialists of the ingenuity of the Creek, he was clear when he said: "We have given to European people on this continent our thought forces. The best blood of our ancestors has been intermingled with their best statesmen and leading citizens. We have ourselves an indestructible element in their natural history. We have shown [that] what they believe to be arid and desert places were habitable and capable of sustaining millions of people. We have led the vanguard of civilization in our conflict with them for tribal existence from ocean to ocean."

What Porter was hinting at was the resilience of his people in the face of the hardship brought by European settlers who had their own, selfish interests. But it was his dreaming that gives the best understanding of what the Creek Nation was before white men's dictatorial rule forced the Creeks to negotiate for their survival with a figurative gun to the head of the Creek Nation. In November 1906, the Senate Select Committee to Investigate Matters Connected with Affairs in the Indian Territory heard this dream from Porter himself:

> In those days they always raised enough to eat and that was
> all we wanted. We had little farms and we raised patches of

corn and potatoes and poultry and pigs, horses and cattle, and a little of everything, and the country was prosperous. In fact, in my early life I don't know that I ever knew of an Indian family that were paupers. There is plenty of them now; there was none then. They were all prosperous and happy and contented in their way, and what more could they want? I say I don't know of an Indian family in my early life that were paupers. In those days the ones that would be paupers if they lived now stayed with their kin folks and they made them work. Now, back of that the custom of the Creeks was that everybody had to work or live on the town, and the town had taskmasters who took care of him and saw that he worked. There was not a skulker or one who shirked amongst us then; quite different from what it is now.

We had a kind of an Arcadian government then. If anyone was sick or unable to work, the neighbors came in and planted his crop, and they took care of it—saw that the fences were all right—and the women took care of the garden, and wood was got for him, and so on. In fact, everything was done under the care of the people—they did everything and looked after the welfare of everything. The Creek had that much knowledge, that they cared for each other in that way; and while they used to live in towns [in Alabama], out here in this peaceful country they had scattered out just like white men, and each one had gone to his farm. . . . In those days you know, a hog ran wild in the woods—went just where he liked—only they would be fed regularly a little corn or something to keep them kind of tame and domesticated; but now you have to keep him under fence, you can't leave him out now like then.

The sheer simplicity of the time was achieved through the resilience of complex cultural norms cultivated over generations. Crops shared. Caring for sick neighbors' crops and their own. The peace and tranquility of an Arcadian life. It is the power of that simplicity that held the memories of what was that propelled them to never let go of what life could be for them.

As white settlers moved into different parts of what was former Creek territory—parts of Florida, Alabama, Georgia, and the Carolinas—Indigenous refugees fled to other parts of the Creek Nation and integrated their traditions into those of the Creek Nation. What was originally the Muskogee then absorbed the Alabamas, Koasatas, Hitchitees, and Tuskegees.

Long before the Creeks were given what Angie Debo called the "perilous gift of American citizenship," they had their own order and structure. Creeks had two primary parts of their government, one that recognized peace and another that recognized war. Peace towns were called White towns and the war towns were known as Red towns. Each town was normally located along the bends and curves of a river or creek to ensure adequate water supply and ample game and hunting opportunities. Cultivation and preservation were skills the Creek practiced long before the term "social movement" was invented. Locations of these towns were responsive to their impact on the environment—abandoning certain towns because of "exhaustion of the fields, outbreak of a pestilence," according to Debo. The Creek were not only industrious, they were also flexible, as the relative size and importance of every town changed based on need. The smaller towns and villages formed around larger towns, setting up independent town councils and ceremonies. Creek towns were "named from historic events, as Nuyaka (often spelled New Yorker) received its name when some of the chiefs signed a treaty at New York," but most town names, "like Concharty (red earth), Wewoka (barking or roaring water), and Tallasi (old or abandoned town)," described a location.

Colonizers often tell themselves stories that the places they have colonized were in desperate need of saving—that their colonizing was redemptive. Or at least that's what I learned in school. But despite what I learned in school, civilization was in Creek lands long before colonial settlers believed that it was. The Creeks long had policies of governance, peace, war, and treaties. They knew what it meant to organize civilization from the highest levels of governance down to the most specific and granular of details.

The private dwellings of each town were grouped around a public space consisting of three units known as the chunkey yard, the chokofa, and the square. These were laid out with ceremonial exactness and were swept and kept in order by individuals appointed for the purpose.

In each town were councils. In times of peace, they held their council meetings in White towns, where they discussed adopting conquered tribes, enacting non-war-related laws, and regulating their governments. These White towns were considered sites of refuge, and aside from enemies of the Creek Nation, no blood was to be spilled in them. Even conquered tribes usually were integrated into White towns. The Creek knew the difference between peace and comity and war, strife, and conflict. For the Red towns, councils focused on war, diplomatic affairs, and foreign policy.

Every one of these towns had focal points of freedom and of "abundant living—of toils shared in careless fellowship, of feasting, dance, and frolic, of sin and retribution and moral aspiration—all directed by the grave voice of the men in council." Creek traditions were centered in a kinship that seemingly could cross tribal barriers and embrace other tribes into its traditions, policies, and spirituality. People the European colonists once called savage had firmly established their own brand of civilization, creating peace and accommodating different perspectives, races, and religions long before Europeans cravenly landed on America's shores.

I GREW UP being taught that the nation's modernization was the most recent accomplishment of landed, Westernized elite men. But the lives of the Creek were led with a level of skill untouched by, not born from, Western influence. Their lives were not about survival, as they would later become. Their lives were about abundance.

But then came survival of a different sort for the Creeks to contend with: the survival of white supremacy.

The United States was not particularly interested in this curious assemblage of kinship that characterized the Creeks and other Indigenous peoples. You cannot abolish bonds of kinship cemented in faith, religion, culture, tradition, and laws. But a nation? A nation can be destroyed. One nation can establish laws and rules that divide members of another nation who once considered each other family. A nation can be negotiated with—not always in good faith—and not be subject to the principles of love and friendship that permeated this kinship. As a result, Creek towns were no longer strictly centers of culture and family and togetherness; they became capitals

that Europeans would visit, prospect, and negotiate. The moment
these Creek towns and their ways of life became subject to the ambitions of their white peers working for another government, the goal
of white supremacy was to ensure that, as Cheryl Harris thought,
"only white possession and occupation of land [could be] validated."
Creek life that had been theirs for generations was being invalidated
by the growing American nation.

I may not know the exact origin of the conventions and quirks
of my Jamaican American identity, but I know that what makes it
akin to the origins of Cow Tom's Black Creek heritage is that it was
formed and forged in the seemingly engulfing fire of white supremacy and its "civilizing" tendencies.

CHAPTER 3

BENJAMIN HAWKINS:
AGENT OF CIVILIZATION

After all the "civilizing" work of their missionaries and
agents, they remained to the end essentially unchanged,
and their hope of survival still rested upon the
unyielding tenacity of their native traits.

ANGIE DEBO

L et us start at what some might call the beginning—a beginning before Cow Tom began. Because Cow Tom didn't become
who he was by accident or happenstance.

It is believed that one of the very first encounters between members of what would be the Creek Nation and Africans was through
Spanish explorer Hernando de Soto, who made his way to North
America in the sixteenth century. De Soto came to America long
before any rock called Plymouth became famous, and long before

the leaders of the thirteen colonies decided that those colonies needed to form a nation. But when de Soto came to America, he brought with him Africans—whom he oppressed as slaves. When they arrived, in approximately 1530, many Africans fled the expedition and took refuge with Indigenous populations and tribes along what today is known as the U.S. part of the Gulf of Mexico. The Coosa tribe in particular resided along the banks of what is now the Mississippi coastline. The tribe saw the actions of these Spanish expeditions—killing, pillaging, and raping—and what was clear to the Coosa, who would be part of what became the Creek Nation, was that the Black people who accompanied these Spanish explorers were not the danger. No, they could potentially be allies against the Spanish, pushing back against the tyranny the explorers exacted upon the Coosa. And though not all these Africans were slaves, they saw the peaceful life among the Coosa and knew the dangers of life under Spanish explorers.

Even if most of the Africans in de Soto's expedition had once been slaves of the Spanish, they did not enter the Coosa tribe as slaves. Reports from de Soto's chronicles show that some slaves took wives in the Coosa. Others were accepted as fugitives from the Spanish and ended up living out the rest of their lives peacefully among the Coosa.

Servitude and slavery did exist in the Creek Nation before African slaves made their way to its shores, but this slavery resembled "kinship slavery," which also existed in West Africa, where slavery was not hereditary or particularly coercive. Such slaves were not bound to a plantation or an owner. Besides, Creek land was communal and its harvest was for the public benefit. Instead, slaves or servants, Black or not, in the earlier forms of the Creek Nation built homes, tilled land, and minded cattle cooperatively.

And to be clear: Creek slaves at this time under kinship slavery were Black, white, and Indian, and each of them had the chance to become Creek through adoption and would never bear the stain of slavery thereafter. And once married to a Creek woman, a slave would no longer be considered a slave and their children would not be the children of slaves or slaves themselves. They would get to be what so few children of color get to be even today: just kids. Once a person was accepted into the family, the markers of ownership faded. Now, this isn't to say that slavery of any kind was or should ever be acceptable. Rather, that the distinctions led to differentiated experiences.

In later years Creeks were so discomfited by the way American plantation owners treated their slaves that historian Claudio Saunt recalled that Creeks were afraid their own townships would some-how become "contaminated through contact with the oppression they observed there." Gary Zellar wrote, "On the plantations [the Creeks] saw African and Indian people bound in iron chains, signi-fying the ultimate power to coerce, an utterly alien concept to Creek traditions of dispersed authority."

As generations unfolded, a group of Black Creeks had themselves (or their ancestors had) worked as slaves for the English, French, and Spanish; these Black Creeks could work as translators, making them invaluable cultural brokers. They often negotiated treaties and agree-ments on behalf of the Creek, as Cow Tom later did. As more and more white settlers made their way to North America, Black Creeks became fixtures in broader Creek life.

How did the Creek go from the Nation that once repulsed the very notion of slavery to one that embraced it? How did Black people whose ancestry could be traced to early iterations of the Creek Nation nearly four hundred years before their expulsion become candidates for having their citizenship nullified?

Usually answers to these questions include long lists of names, consequences of policy decisions, and a collection of random unexpectedly important events. And yes, in this case, there are also several partial answers. But in the case of the Creeks and the Blacks, the blame can be placed on the concerted effort of "civilization" and its forefather: Benjamin Hawkins.

IT WAS 1805. By now, the Creeks could no longer stand neutral between the French and the British. With first the French out of North America and then the British out of the American colonies, the United States had begun to expand its own government. States started to cede some of their autonomy to this new national government as it strengthened its federal bona fides, including giving control of dealing with Native Americans to the U.S. government, setting in motion a path for one of the most influential and least known leaders in American history.

This wunderkind was unlike his modern contemporaries in that he had no pedigree and no lofty education and was a member of no political family. Yet he had the ear of the first four presidents of the United States.

Born in 1754 to Philemon Hawkins, an officer during the Revolutionary War, Benjamin attended the College of New Jersey, which later became Princeton. When the Revolutionary War broke out in

1775, Hawkins, a polyglot, was dispatched at age twenty as a colonel to serve as General George Washington's interpreter, representing Washington in almost all dealings with the French.

After he served in the Continental Army, Hawkins went into politics. By age thirty, he had been elected to the North Carolina House of Representatives and served one year before North Carolina sent Hawkins to Congress in the 1780s to determine how the disparate states could consolidate power during America's early fits and starts. While there, Hawkins witnessed the earliest drafts of and debates over the U.S. Constitution.

His work for North Carolina earned him a spot as a delegate to the state constitutional convention in 1789 in Fayetteville, where he and the other attendees ratified the U.S. Constitution. And in the same year, without any official party affiliation, Hawkins earned a seat in the U.S. Senate at thirty-five years old. This overachiever was a year younger than John F. Kennedy when he became a senator, eight years younger than Barack Obama, and nine years younger than Cory Booker.

His political prowess helped him keep pace with the growing United States. From his birth to the end of his Senate term in 1795, the population of the United States exploded by 83 percent. Two states, Vermont and Kentucky, were added to the United States. More wars had been fought and won. Trade with Britain had been normalized with the passage of the Jay Treaty. And Hawkins's own state opened the first state university in America, the University of North Carolina. As a senator, Hawkins touched nearly every aspect of these transformational moments during the nation's early history.

But Hawkins's most pivotal career ascent was to come.

. . .

By October 7, 1805, Hawkins had completed his Senate term, returned to the Deep South, and used slaves to build and run a plantation in Georgia. While his elected work might have been over, Hawkins wasn't done with working on behalf of the U.S. government. That month, Hawkins returned to Washington to report on the work he had been doing. *The Augusta Herald* depicted him as a hero, noting, "It will afford pleasure to a benevolent mind to know that the efforts of Colonel Hawkins to meliorate the condition of the savage tribes, and to bring them into something like a social state, have been greatly successful and that they are almost daily, though slowly, making advances in civilization."

The article's author expanded on the austere order and prosperity Hawkins was destined to bring these "savages": "The plough and the hoe are now also in very general use among them, and in becoming attached to property and being acquainted with the comforts and advantages of agricultural improvements, they are losing very considerably that predilection for the chase and hunting life, which almost universally characterizes savage nations."

To the nineteenth-century writer for the Georgia newspaper, there was almost nothing worth keeping about this way of life—hunting and chasing—that would be part of this young country's promising path to progress. No, the habits and happenings of these "savages" had to change in their estimation. And Benjamin Hawkins was the right man for the job. In fact, "there can be little doubt that a foundation is laid for an entire change in the disposition and habits of these tribes."

Hawkins's challenge was clear: to solve the "Indian Problem" on behalf of the United States government.

DURING HIS TIME IN CONGRESS, Hawkins had negotiated several treaties with the Creek Nation that ate into its territory in places like Georgia, where the Creek held most of the western part of the state. He knew the negotiating tactics of the Creeks and understood the familial structure of their governance. He knew their laws, customs, and traditions at least well enough for General Washington to appoint him as the federal government's principal agent for the Creeks in 1786.

Hawkins's work with the Creeks made him invaluable not just to Washington when Washington became president in 1789 but also to the next three presidents Hawkins would serve: John Adams, Thomas Jefferson, and James Madison. He convinced a busy President Washington to weigh in on negotiating the landmark Treaty of New York, which allowed the Creeks to defend their lands from white prospectors who tried to build homesteads on lands the Creeks had held long before white men made their way to America. How gracious of the U.S. government to allow the Creek to defend the land they always had from prospectors who wanted to lay claim to what wasn't theirs. He also led two other Indian agents in telling the Choctaw Nation what the borders would be between Choctaw land and U.S. land.

Hawkins succeeded because he helped execute the marching orders of white supremacy: minimize the distinctions of others into discrete buckets that could never contain the great beauty of their backgrounds, civilized or savage. Put another way, Hawkins made possible a dangerous and inevitable trap veiled as a choice for the Creek: either participate in the means of U.S. civilization to dismantle Indigenous institutions, customs, and traditions, or reject the U.S. civilization and have their future determined without their input and accept an accelerated destruction of these institutions, customs, and traditions. So it is no surprise that people like Hawkins were deemed successful for carrying the torch of civilization. White, European civilization.

These "successes," especially with the Native American Nations to which Hawkins was assigned, were well documented—often by Hawkins himself. From 1796 to 1806 he wrote hundreds of letters. The recipients were some of the biggest power brokers in early American politics, on topics including nearly every business dealing, U.S.-tribal interactions, and almost all his personal dealings. He wrote letters to presidents, generals, other Indian agents, leaders of Native American Nations, and the tribes within those Nations. His diplomatic prowess was unquestioned.

But back to the "Indian Problem."

Imagine millions of acres of plush lands near bodies of water with beautiful embankments and gulfs that welcome the warm waters of the Atlantic Ocean. These lands served as the unwelcome yet profitable landing pads for thousands of enslaved Africans who would produce the capital at nearly no cost that would line the landowners' pockets. The paradoxically free blood money bought with Black lives built prestigious universities that generally did not welcome the very people who built them, built the White House, built the nation's capital city. The nation that fought valiantly against the tyranny of the British is hobbling through its infancy, trying to figure out what it can be. States like Georgia, Florida, and the Carolinas, and the territories that will soon become the states of Alabama and Mississippi, have untold riches that only explorers, pioneers, and adventurers could just barely begin to comprehend or articulate.

But his new nation's leaders made deals with the people they still call savages, often to their faces. These people hold that land legally, but these leaders know that they can always change the laws upon which those treaties were made. These people have what you want, and by the rules of white supremacy, the nation's leaders, these white men, believe they have a right to them. They see these "savages" as working to "equally distribute the land and live happy lives," as Pleasant Porter would put it, instead of instilling private ownership, building plantations with slaves, and dividing labor. White Christian missionaries do what Jesus would not do: Instead of loving Native people with an unending reservoir of compassion, they try to change the very characteristics of Creek culture.

What do they do to get states to listen to the will of the federal government? They tame and civilize the savages. Subject them to the sort of cultural, economic, and political structures government leaders were desperate to execute themselves. And when they had developed their land, they bought it on the cheap and forced Native people off it in order to build for themselves the shining city on a hill they think America is.

That is "civilization."

FOR DECADES, George Washington has been recognized as the most popular president in American history. And why not? He led the Continental Army to an unlikely triumph against the British army. He accepted the difficult task of leading the newly formed

United States as its first president in its consolidation of federal power among the states. He led when most did not want to. And he resisted the usual human urge for unending power by stepping down after two terms. But he, like many politicians of yesteryear, benefits from our country's penchant for forgetting the critical history to instead portray leaders we have grown to revere in the ways we want them to be remembered.

But those who were here first, those of us who came later with darker complexions and were made to live lives at the margin because we had to be three fifths of a person to compromise with Southern slaveholders and their Northern sympathizers, might instead call him what the Iroquois did: Conotocaurius, or "Town Destroyer."

With the ascent of George Washington came the ascent of his protégé, Benjamin Hawkins. Like many other white, newly called Americans, Washington and Hawkins saw tribal nations as a problem. With the Spanish and the French both on their way out and with the British vanquished, the new United States itched to expand. But standing in the way of satisfying that itch were thousands of families who were there before the white men invaded their lands. These families, Indian Nations, were the obstacle to white men's claim to the unknown opportunities that lay beyond.

So early in Washington's first term, Hawkins came up with a plan to place the Nations under the protection of the U.S. government in hopes of "civilizing and modernizing their societies." This plan to "improve Native American society" was not meant to improve Native Americans for the benefit of Native Americans. It was to teach them to become more white, more American. It meant that the Creek and others would have to shed what made them Creek and accept the traits that would make them "American": to become more white than they could be or wanted to be.

This idea was championed by Washington and his secretary of war, Henry Knox. They were eager, even desperate, to open new lands beyond the thirteen states, no matter who had been there first. But they needed to prime these "savages" to prepare them for the profit-motivated reasons of white intrusion.

So they civilized them.

While the government's publicly stated motive may have been to train Native Americans in the European skills of cultivating land, farming, and developing industries best suited to their connection to the land, its real goal was to instill Western civilization's notion of private ownership in Native populations.

By establishing the idea of private lands, and with Native Americans no longer hunting as they once did, the United States could settle, over time, Native peoples on smaller land plots, divide them, and prepare them for the eventual private sales of their lands. Never mind the fact that for centuries before white men ever arrived, Native American Nations, including the Creek, had been cultivating the land and governing themselves peacefully and equitably. They just did so in ways that did not resonate with European conventions. Bartering, exchanging, developing cash crops, and settling land to ranch communally and with greater intentionality toward sustainability were conventions of many Native Americans.

It was here that Benjamin Hawkins rose to the occasion. His relationship with Washington and his prowess as a political leader at the local, state, and federal levels made him the perfect candidate to train Native people in how to live like white settlers. He started with the Creeks.

He began by making nice with Creek leaders: attending community meetings, gatherings, and celebrations. Some of his bosses were puzzled by these actions. President Thomas Jefferson wrote a letter to Hawkins in 1803 warning him of severe concerns that he and other leaders had that the interests of Georgians might be more "attached to the interests of the Indians than of the United States." To be clear, Hawkins's job, which Jefferson lauded as "indefatigable and successful," was in Jefferson's words "the attainment of . . . peace and lands and it is essential that our agent acquire that sort of influence over the Indians." He was the go-to for the U.S. government for instilling peace by way of civilizing the savage and crafting a path for the U.S. geographic footprint to grow, even if that print lay on the necks of Creeks.

Hawkins quickly became the most sought-after political leader for businessmen and politicians alike on all matters Creek and their lands. On February 2, 1797, William Panton, the Scottish founder of Panton, Leslie & Company, one of the country's largest trading firms, which had worked in Spanish Florida and owned nineteen land grants on which more than 250 slaves worked, wrote to Hawkins:

> In the course of my tour through the Creeks, I find that you
> have a very extensive commercial intercourse with them,
> and that probably your present or future prospects may be
> materially affected by the political state of affairs in Eu
> rope. I do not know that I can in any way contribute any
> thing that may be of service to you, within my agency, but
> if you know wherein I can, and will do me the favour to call
> on me, I possess the decision, and will prove to you my
> readiness to assist you.

This is the modern equivalent of a Fortune 500 CEO currying the favor of a new secretary of state as the secretary tries to sort out the issues that will affect the CEO's business interests. Panton had done this before, presenting gifts to the Creek Nation on behalf of the British Crown. His work with the Creeks and other Nations had made him wealthy and his company the largest mercantile company in the southeastern United States.

Not only did Hawkins greatly influence the economic and social future of the Creeks, he took a wife who many say was a Creek woman and named two of his children after the Muskogee tribe and Cherokee. American leaders at the time considered him a "friend of the Indian." In truth, he was no friend at all. What to some might have seemed like a white man bestowing onto "savages" tools to update and modernize their way of life was actually Hawkins working to crater the very future of the Creeks—and, as a consequence, of the Black people who also made Creek country home.

On March 7, 1797, Hawkins wrote to Timothy Barnard, a Scottish trader. He lived in the Creek Nation and had married a Yuchi (a tribe within the Creek Nation) woman, and their son Timpoochee would one day run the Yuchi tribe and sit on the Creek National Council. Barnard had recently been appointed Hawkins's interpreter to the Creeks, and Hawkins had a list of directives for him.

"[First] inform the Indians of the fixture of the posts on their lands in conformity with the arrangements made with them at Colerain." The Treaty of Colerain allowed the U.S. government to dictate the boundary lines of Creek territory and that large trading posts would sit on Creek land to harvest all the potential benefits of Creek land with no cut for the Creek. Hawkins's first dictate was to remind the Creeks that U.S. economic interests were here to stay.

Later in the letter Hawkins directed Barnard to "inform the Indians of the complaints sent in by the Governor of this State [Georgia] to the President, and the whole nation ought to be under serious apprehensions for their future tranquility unless a stop can be put to such abominable proceedings on the part of their young men." Creek men had continued to hunt as they always had, the way they knew to live abundantly on land they knew as their own, which didn't sit well with their white "civilizing peace-givers." Even today, when white families see faces unlike their own doing what they have always done, "their future tranquility" is jostled and they clutch their metaphorical pearls. Hawkins doubled down on the unjustified fear that white people had and have of those nonwhite people: savages causing trouble.

> One thing above all others you are to be particularly attentive to: The Indians are, as you know, beggars, and have not the shadow of gratitude for any favours they receive, almost everything is lost on them. Their annuity will be punctually paid, but they are not to be suffered to expect to obtain presents of any kind whatever when they visit our posts. They must in future be treated as men, and not as spoiled children. Those who are in the Indian department must expect to live on their salaries, and for them to do the business assigned them, and must exhibit in their own conduct at all times, examples worthy of imitation to the Indians. I have come to correct abuses and to fix the management of Indian affairs in those who will zealously and steadily execute the orders of the government.

In other words, after ravaging their lands, minimizing their territory, and conscripting them into wars they bore no responsibility for, the U.S. government, by way of Hawkins's dictates, expected the Indigenous to demonstrate gratitude. They were supposed to pick themselves up by their proverbial bootstraps, even if the bootstraps they once had were stolen to become the bootstraps of their colonial counterparts.

In a letter to Timpoochee the next day, Hawkins writes again that these "spoiled children" and "unruly young men have done mischief [by continuing to live in America as Creek]." But in a quip, Hawkins undoes any measure of independence in the Creek leadership by saying, "You and the other chiefs will take measure to govern the nation." Chiefs had become subjects and dispensers of the United States' notions of justice.

In other letters, Hawkins tried to convey his "sincere wishes for the prosperity of your nation," and he hoped that Timpoochee would "believe me to be your friend." It was a refrain repeated by the U.S. government just before the hammer fell on any true expression of friendship.

But how many friends write to friends of color—Indigenous friends—conveying threats?

On April 3, 1797, Hawkins wrote to Creek chief Efau Tustunnagau to deliver a clear threat. First, he told Efau that he would need to "order as many of your young men as you deem necessary to accompany the Sergeant to this post" to do what was called a land line run, to mark the ever-decreasing size of Creek Nation territory. Next, Hawkins made sure the chief understood what kind of man he was dealing with: "You have had an opportunity to see the supreme executive of the United States and many of my fellow citizens, and I hope you have formed just conceptions of the power as well as justice of our government, and that you will on all occasions impress on the minds of your countrymen the information you have received on these points, and how necessary it is to your existence as a nation to cultivate a friendly intercourse with us by a strict compliance with the terms of your treaty."

Hawkins, the man who came to "manage Indian affairs" and civilize the Creek, was actually on a mission to undo the Creek and erode the very imprint of Creek life on this country's lands.

What did this look like in practice?

Creeks were often strong-armed into selling their lands to the U.S. government. With that money, Hawkins then "strongly encouraged" the Creeks to buy tools for the advancement of their economy: plows, hoes, looms, cotton gins, spinning wheels, machinery, and blacksmith tools. In agriculture, Creek women were indispensable, as they usually ran the farming, planting rice, corn, beans, and squash. However, he also introduced them to producing and cultivating cotton at commercial scale, and he encouraged them to focus their farming efforts to produce cotton.

Hawkins and his team also introduced Creek women to spinning and weaving, showing the women a preference for European-manufactured cloth materials and the machines to make the materials more efficiently. Hawkins took traditions of finger-weaving that had been passed down through generations and replaced them with "efficiency." Even though they could still make cloth by finger-weaving fibers, the Creek began to prefer European-manufactured cloth, which they had been buying since it first became available more than a century earlier. They now had the necessary machinery to make this cloth more efficiently, thus freeing them from having to purchase it.

Controversial conservative economist Thomas Sowell once summed up the essential characteristics of any economy: "The most basic question is not what is best, but who shall decide what is best." In the case of the Creeks, Hawkins took the opportunity to decide what was best without questioning whether he or the U.S. government had the right to do so for those who didn't ask for their help.

The civilization plan that rocked Creek life further was the effort to intentionally suppress the hunting habits of Creek men. Hawkins and his acolytes taught that hunting was not as economically productive as farming. But cultural meaning was not nearly as valuable as the material output the Creeks could produce—not just for themselves but for the rising needs of the growing U.S. population. For the Creeks, hunting epitomized maleness and manhood. Nearly every time Creek land was ceded or coercively sold to the U.S. government, Creeks, especially the men, knew that both their land and their culture, especially hunting, were dwindling fast. Hunting lands were disappearing into the hands of a fast-growing country whose government felt as if its expanding destiny was made manifest.

Long before Hawkins came into Creek life, the Creeks were ranching, but ranching communally. There had long been Creek families who owned cattle of some kind. In some cases, this was for ranching; many families kept cows and hogs to provide food for their families and communities collectively. The nudging of European "civilization" and settlers directed Creeks to sell their cattle to buy more guns, cloth, and even African slaves—a practice one cannot find much in Creek country before the Revolutionary War.

To make the Creeks accept ranching, the minimization of

hunting, the ceding of land, and the formal introduction to enslaving Black people, Hawkins and the U.S. government knew that the concept of private property must take hold. They knew that communalism among the Creeks provided strength, but you can divide and conquer a nation more easily with private property if you pit family estate against family estate. With private property, Creek families adopted capitalism, and rough sketches of class divisions started to emerge. Such civilization sent ripples throughout Creek country and culture that would forever change this land and what it meant to be not white in America.

Hawkins was an effective agent. He did his job and secured the trust of four presidents, running the bureaus that administered operations in each of the Five Tribes. The Five Tribes—Cherokee, Choctaw, Chickasaw, Creek, and Seminole—occupied large swaths of what Angie Debo called "great fertile land" in what is now the southeastern United States.

Though Hawkins worked more than two centuries ago, his impact on race in America is still being felt today, particularly by people like the Simmons family. Civilization was just a not-so-subtle term for making America white.

The enduring legacy of white supremacy is that it creates and calcifies categories—often artificial ones—to divide, conquer, and eventually subjugate. Perhaps Hawkins, in his grand vision for the Creek Nation, did not intend to create the path for proliferating slavery through the corridors of Creek life. But intent will never matter as much as the impact that actions have.

Slavery, especially chattel slavery (the practice of enslaving and owning human beings and their offspring as property, able to be bought, sold, and forced to work without wages, as distinguished from other systems of forced, unpaid, or low-wage labor also considered to be slavery), in the land of the Creek was something that the U.S. government fostered and encouraged. The Creeks did not want it, and when they eventually adopted slavery, it was because they were being "civilized" and resisting civilization could come with dangers too great.

Imagine you're Creek in the late 1700s and early 1800s and you have been forced to accept the tenets of capitalism and the rugged individualism that comes with it. The people who introduced you to these concepts are growing in number at a rate you likely did not expect when they first appeared and imposed themselves on your land. They tell you that you no longer are communally linked to the people you consider family and are now a private citizen of a nation you didn't agree to belong to. You are competing against them now. And they tell you that there are people from Africa who have helped to generate massive sums of wealth for white people at no cost because these people from Africa by law aren't fully people and don't have to be paid. Now wealth is the way to outpace everyone else in a community that's becoming less communal. Slavery, as detestable as Claudio Saunt said it was to the Creek, became a means of trying to win in a new world that said winning as an individual—not as a community, a people, a family—was the only way to win.

Before Hawkins's racial capitalism took hold among Creeks, they did not see much inherent need to use coerced labor. Subsistence farming and hunting were intrinsically Creek and male. So the use of slave labor did not much matter before the introduction of commercial agriculture that Hawkins and the rest of the U.S. government thought would be important for civilizing the Creeks.

Hawkins helped to introduce and encourage this practice even further. According to historian Gary Zellar, chattel slavery did not really exist within the Creek Nation prior to the Revolutionary War. But Hawkins was concerned that Creeks did not know how to "properly manage their slave property," while praising Creeks who "employed slave labor in commercial agriculture." Hawkins and the plan for civilization made America's use of slavery as a tactic of reducing labor costs clear to the Creeks. During the Revolutionary War, the British would present African slaves to the Creeks as gifts when tribes within the Creek Nation cooperated with them.

As the United States established its foothold in this new land, slavery became more pervasive in the Creek Nation, but it took several forms. Slavery in some Creek families resembled the sort of chattel slavery one found on the plantations of white people. Slavery status became hereditary, with slave quarters built on the back lots of large plantations. Other Creek families held slaves but lived with them at near parity, sharing tasks and frequently dining with them. Some historians have found that many Creek families had a "patron-client" relationship with their slaves. Slaves would provide for themselves, work the land, and provide a kickback of their earnings to their owners. This patron-client system of slavery allowed Black Creek families to build out long-term generational ties with the Creek Nation. And with patron-client relationships intact, agreements existed between slaves and slaveholders to not sell slaves without first obtaining their permission.

With the intentional decline of farming, hunting, deerskin trade, and more, slaves served an ever-growing importance in Creek life. Prior to Hawkins's involvement in their lives, the Creeks excelled at subsistence farming but did not have the knowledge or experience to transition easily into the commercial agriculture they were being forced into. With the introduction of slaves, Creek slaveholders became more effective at commercial agriculture.

The demand for commercial agriculture, pumped by the fuel of civilization and powered by white supremacy, created indelible divisions between Creek and Black, making those who were Black less Creek than they could be. Hawkins's civilizing made less civil and worthy of civility the Blacks who were also Creek.

But Hawkins's impact did not stop at slavery. The danger of civilizing people whose land you want is that eventually you need them to leave so that you can take their land. For the Creeks, removal was not far away.

THE PLAN OF CIVILIZATION split Creek opinion. There was no mistaking among Creeks that "civilization" was code for priming their land to be overtaken by the federal government through land acquisition. Some thought this was how Creek life would survive: by accommodating. Others saw American civilization as destruction. Most saw civilization as both. In order to prevent violence against the Creek Nation by the U.S. government—in other words, to survive—the Creeks needed to comply with white civilization. But doing that set Creek life on a slippery slope toward destruction.

In 1813, the tense divide between factions erupted into a civil war known as the Creek War or the Red Stick War. The Red Sticks, an assembly of Creek rebels, sought to tear down every expression of America and the civilization that had infiltrated Creek life. They destroyed tools bought by the coerced sale of Creek lands. They killed cattle that Creek families raised in the way this new country had instructed them to do. But instead of letting the supposedly independent Creek Nation sort out its own issues, the United States got involved. General Andrew Jackson commanded a fleet of seven thousand American troops against the Red Stick army of four thousand. When Jackson and his army defeated the Creeks in August 1814, he negotiated the signing of the Treaty of Fort Jackson, which forced Creeks to surrender nearly twenty-one million acres of land in parts of what is now Georgia and Alabama.

Twenty-one million acres lost introduced a swift economic implosion and laid the groundwork for what came next.

Over the next several years there was much debate in Congress over whether the federal government should stick with its policy of "civilizing" away their so-called "Indian Problem" or carve a new path of removing their "Indian Problem" altogether. When Andrew Jackson was elected president in 1828, he pushed for a new approach to the "Indian Problem": move them west of the Mississippi. In 1830 the passage of the Indian Removal Act made his wishes law.

From the Great Smoky Mountain ranges of North Carolina and Tennessee to the Gulf shores of Florida, Alabama, and Mississippi to the rolling hills of Georgia, the Creeks' land had been vast and communal. Yes, they warred, but they also knew peace and institutionalized both peace and war. Their land was prime in its abundance and fertility, and their expertise at maintaining it and their ability to sustain all that they cultivated seemed endless.

The Creek, like the rest of the Five Tribes, were forced off the "great fertile land" for white settlers to acquire and transform. But when Jackson moved them west, he did so with the intent that this move would be the last. The agreement reached between the U.S.

government and the Creeks was that the land beyond the Mississippi was supposed to be the Creeks' and no one else's. But treaties with Indigenous populations seemed as if they were crafted only to be broken.

Along the Trail of Tears—the forced removal of approximately one hundred thousand Native Americans from the Southeast to what became known as Indian Territory—was a young Black man named Cow Tom. He had been "civilized" by way of being born Black, a putative slave, and now "removed"—marginalized by his Blackness, not just by an identity of slave that his descendants today still rebuff, but by an Indigeneity that set him, as Debo would later write, on a road to disappearance. The invention and civilization of the Creek Nation and their removal forged Cow Tom's identity. His long march west with Chief Yargee would set the stage for a fight against the white supremacy that empowered white men to look at Creek land and think, "This is now ours."

This is where the story of Cow Tom begins— at the end of a brutal march west with no clear vision of what was to come.

CHAPTER 4

COW TOM BUILDS A HOME

That is what Black reincarnation is. The debt is still owed.
We keep making generations to collect our inheritance.
There isn't much agreement about what that inheritance is
though. I will admit that to you. We are American,
profoundly so. Its scullery maids and its children.
Offspring of this beautiful ugly nation.

IMANI PERRY

My parents had been drawing up a will. And they wanted to talk about it—with all of their children.

What surprised me about this unexpected news wasn't that the will forced us to discuss money—of which there was not much—but how it obliged us to talk about our pasts: my parents', their parents', and so on.

Despite the uncomfortable trappings that accompany end-of-life conversations, my parents seemed downright eager to talk. Here was a chance, at last, to compel their children to hear how our lives fit into their lives and those of their ancestors. What they felt they owed their elders and what they felt their elders had given them.

Inheritances can be strange. But talking about inheritances is always strange. Determining who gets what inevitably makes everyone think about death. And talking about death is never welcome, especially when no one has died.

Of course, my Jamaican American parents brought up the subject of their will and their kids' inheritance right after we finished opening presents on December 25, 2018. That's right: on Christmas Day.

I can't blame them; no one really can. My grandmother's lucidity disappeared near the beginning of that year. And none of her finances were in order. Her husband—my grandfather, who had died seven years earlier—had been a pastor of a church in the South Bronx for nearly forty years. And the church building he left her had debts and payments that hadn't been settled. In the church, the rows of chairs remained where the former congregants had left them when the church closed its door fifteen years earlier. My grandmother's home, which sat on the border of Brownsville and East Flatbush in Brooklyn, where my father was raised and where I was babysat, housed tenants, both literal and figurative: a family of four on the top floor, one of my aunts in the basement studio, and memories in every crevice and corner of the three-floor walk-up. The disposition of neither the house nor the church had been set down in a will. So when Grandma was no longer lucid, my father, mother, aunts, and uncles did what they had to do to get Grandma's affairs in order. And my parents wrote a will.

None of Grandma's kids will get big paydays when she passes.

After funeral costs, the second mortgage on the home, and some miscellaneous bills, the will won't have much there there.

Perhaps the lack of money in Grandma's estate motivated my parents to give us this odd Christmas present: their will. And with the presentation of that will came a long, awkward conversation not just about their inevitable deaths but also about their pasts. The talk spanned where they came from, what had been sacrificed to set aside more money in their will than my grandmother had, and why they were "happily obligated" to preserve these resources for us, their three children, all now adults.

The awkwardness of this conversation truly set in when I considered that my financial fate—crafted through my parents' better fortunes—would be different from many of the very people who look like me: Black folk.

Only a few weeks earlier, I sat in a Harvard Kennedy School classroom, where a professor presented data that showed that the average white family had forty-one times as much wealth as the average Black family. During this class, Race and Inequality in American Democracy, we discussed how this 2016 study showed that it would take 228 years for Black families to gain the same wealth as their white counterparts. That is a far longer time than we are today from the Declaration of Independence. What financial legacy can Black families hope to leave if the average Black family has $3,500 in wealth and is twice as likely as a white family to have zero or negative net worth?

While my dad made the legalese of their will digestible—showing how lucky they were, as Black parents, to leave some money for their children—all I could think about was the story of another Black man, a Black man who left more than the memories of his existence to his children.

His name was—is—Cow Tom. He inspired me because he achieved what we might call his American Dream not in America: He built his inheritance in "Indian Country," leaving for his Black Creek family wealth, social prominence, and bona fide citizenship. He left his family grist mills, cattle, and land—in total worth $50,000, or more than $1.1 million in today's dollars. At the time, it must have been seen as a staggering fortune, one that still outpaces the wealth of Black people today. But the color of Cow Tom's skin sealed his fate in the eyes of a white man who recorded part of his history. His Blackness made him someone's negro—his value relegated to the power of someone not Black.

BY 1842, at age forty-four, Ethan Allen Hitchcock had reached the rank of lieutenant colonel in the U.S. Army. Hitchcock, a Vermont native, was the son of Judge Samuel Hitchcock, who had been the first attorney general of Vermont and a U.S. district judge. His mother was the daughter of Ethan Allen, the famed Revolutionary War hero who founded the state of Vermont and led the Green Mountain Boys to recapture land from the British. Hitchcock's siblings would go on to become a state supreme court justice and a legendary attorney. And his nephew and namesake would become the U.S. secretary of the interior who would preside over the reorganization of Native American life.

High-level government service and military excellence were in Hitchcock's blood. But so were diligence and an eye for detail. Hitchcock kept a diary where he recorded his daily activities, almost without fail. He labeled the top of his pages with the date, and right under the date he penned "morning" or "evening." As if he knew that almost two hundred years later, someone would study his diary.

As a leader in the Seminole Wars in the first half of the nineteenth century, Hitchcock cultivated relationships with Native American leaders and chronicled his time with them. After the Seminole Wars and before his leadership in the Mexican-American War, Hitchcock toured parts of Indian Territory (in what is now Oklahoma). He was there to ferret out details on fraud perpetrated on the Five Tribes. It had been rumored that contractors working in Indian Territory used dubious practices to profit personally and unfairly. Hitchcock's observations would later be compiled in a report that Congress tried to repress for more than a year.

While he ruminated in his diary on the graft, corruption, and subversive behavior he uncovered, Hitchcock became friendly with Cat Yargee, an accomplished cattle herder and Creek Nation chief. Yargee spoke no English, some said out of a refusal to adopt non-Creek customs. Many so-called full-blood Creeks adopted this practice of refusing to learn English as a purity test of Creek identity. But Black people within the Creek Nation played a special role in bridging the gap between the Creek world and that of the ever-growing world of this newer, whiter America. In fact, their relationship could only have been fostered by a Black man in the Creek Nation when Hitchcock called Yargee's Black slave and translator his "Negro Tom." Tom, who later became known as Cow Tom for his cattle herding skills, acted as interpreter for the two men.

Hitchcock noted in his diary that Cow Tom, then thirty-two years old, "wants a school for his children" and "wishes he had a grist mill. Thinks the wheelwright employed by the government don't do well." Hitchcock, almost unknowingly, cataloged the dreams of a Black man, someone he could only imagine as a slave. And Cow Tom has been recorded as a former slave while his descendants today contend that he was not—that rather he was in the employ of Yargee and that it was a white gaze that limited who and what Cow Tom was and could be.

But slave or not, someone who is perceived as a slave has limits. Someone whose dreams simply didn't matter, even to a thoughtful man like Hitchcock. One wonders what Hitchcock would have thought if he had lived to see what young Cow Tom became.

Hitchcock's reference to Tom as "Yargee's Negro Tom" has been interpreted to mean that Tom was a slave. But Cow Tom's descendants don't accept that narrative. For Hitchcock, Cow Tom was nothing more than one of Yargee's slaves with pipe dreams about opening a school, owning a grist mill, and building on his land. As an educated, successful white man, how could Hitchcock think of Cow Tom as anything but a slave? How could he imagine Cow Tom being someone whose identity we might easily see in today's world: someone who is both fully Black and fully Creek?

But Cow Tom's jet-black skin, as his grandchildren described it, couldn't make him equal with Yargee, and certainly not with Hitchcock. So Cow Tom remained "his Negro Tom."

This is what white supremacy does: it places limits on who we can be based on oversimplified versions of identity. Identity just becomes a marker determined by its proximity to whiteness. Cow Tom couldn't be anything but a slave in the most conventional chattel slavery way. He couldn't have been a worker on Yargee's estate. For Hitchcock, Cow Tom couldn't have been someone who broke bread with Yargee and was treated as an equal, because Hitchcock was a white man of privilege whose experience didn't reflect that rich complexity.

But who can blame Hitchcock? The Civil War had yet to be fought over the institution of slavery (among many issues). Black people, especially in this part of the country, had almost never experienced freedom. So, interpreter or not, Cow Tom was for Hitchcock simply a slave with wild dreams. His name came with the signifier of ownership: his Negro Tom. And a label of color that Hitchcock likely did not use when describing his white counterparts. It might seem harmless, an oversight even—maybe even well intended. But intention doesn't matter as much as impact. The word of Hitchcock, a white man writing in his journal about Cow Tom, resounds larger than the words of Cow Tom's descendants, who have tracked their lineage and guarded their family's oral tradition carefully.

And to be clear: this is racist.

It is important that we understand what I mean, because I will use the words "racist" and "racism" in a way you might find new. As Ibram Kendi put it, "racist" is "not the worst word in the English language; it is not the equivalent of a slur. It is descriptive, and the only way to undo racism is to consistently identify and describe it—and then dismantle it. The attempt to turn this usefully descriptive term into an almost unusable slur is, of course, designed to do the opposite: to freeze us into inaction." And I do not want to freeze you into inaction.

What Hitchcock did is what has happened to me and to nearly every person of color who fits or refuses to fit into the box that white America created for us. And in these boxes white America superimposed its expectations on us. This happens every time I am asked if

I'm the parking attendant, or the store clerk, or if I'm a professional football player or rapper. This happens every time a parent has a talk with their child of color before they get behind the wheel for the first time.

Hitchcock, as did many other people, likely thought nothing of the label "slave."

And at this point in American history, slavery included more than 3.5 million people, most of whom were kept as chattel, the form of slavery that allowed people to be considered legal property to be bought, sold, and owned forever. It was protected by the U.S. Constitution. And Black people who resided in the United States, free or not, could not vote and were considered three fifths of a white person. In the eyes of white people, Cow Tom could never be anything more than the property of his supposed owner.

In the eyes of my classmates, co-workers, strangers, and neighbors, I could be nothing more than an intimidating Black man. And racism influences why people who look like me are rarely given the benefit of the doubt when interacting with law enforcement today. These kinds of racism influenced the recording of Cow Tom's story as well, and racism continues to influence why his descendants cannot consider themselves Creek, even though a critical and still-binding treaty says they can.

Racism is not pejorative. Identifying racism where we see it, past and present, is just being honest about the history upon which our identity has been established.

Perhaps if Hitchcock had not been racist and if he had lived longer, his expectations for what he considered a slave was capable of would have been shattered by everything Cow Tom accomplished.

And if Hitchcock had been a more attentive student of history, he would have taken more care before he labeled this Cow Tom character a slave.

I GREW UP IN CHURCH. Black church. Old-school Black church. Women wore big hats and hid their ankles out of modesty. Men wore suits with ties. Preachers would whoop. According to CNN journalist John Blake, "Whooping is a celebratory style of black preaching that pastors typically use to close a sermon. Some church scholars compare it to opera; it's that moment the sermon segues into song." At the end of every service during my childhood, my grandfather would remind the congregants that on the other side of this life would be a choice between heaven and a life of eternal damnation in hell. He'd admonish us about a life led on earth that was spent "sinning" without the acceptance of Jesus Christ as our Lord and Savior. He'd tell us that the wages of sin are death.

I wasn't even ten years old when I heard these words, and much of what he said flew over my head. But what I did know was that sin was bad, indescribably so. There was a long list of sins, especially in this predominantly Jamaican storefront church my grandfather pastored. Sex (unless you were married). Liquor (unless it was Guinness stout in the weekly carrot juice drink the older folks in the family made). Add to that list clubs, movie theaters, card games, secular music, and voting for Republicans, along with many others.

The Creek might not have had the same notions of sin I grew up with. But they had the same aversion to what we now call America's original sin: slavery. But any sin—big or small—as I learned growing up, was the highest point on a downward, slippery slope. I learned that one sin, no matter how repugnant it may seem at first, makes the next sin or the expansion of the first sin that much easier to commit.

The Creeks had observed the dangers of this ever-growing trend of slavery around them. Not only did it put the lives of Black men and women at risk, but also it put at risk the Creek way of life. Their community was disrupted. They saw on English and then American plantations not only Blacks but Creeks taken as slaves and traded for more Black slaves, then shipped off to the West Indies. They saw America's original sin up close as they witnessed the intensely brutal and inhumane practice, especially applied by the British.

Creek slave ownership, like most sins, started small and grew over time. It's what the apostle Paul called becoming reprobate—the state in which you start convincing yourself that the thing you once reviled and called sinful is now the very thing you defend. For the Creeks, slavery was a means of surviving. First the British and then the Americans reduced and curtailed the Creeks' hunting grounds and limited where they could go. Successfully hunting game became far more difficult. So some Creeks turned to ranching, a vocation made easier by employing people and made even more profitable by using enslaved ones.

But it is important to remember that slavery in the Creek Nation didn't take hold nearly the way Benjamin Hawkins and others hoped it would. Creeks weren't as interested in accumulating wealth and property as Western colonists were. They planted, harvested, and grew communally. To the Creek, coercion represented some of the evilest human tendencies. Enslaving Blacks so that they could make products more cheaply to earn for their families alone and not the community did not initially take hold at a broad level. Instead, according to historian Claudio Saunt, "the vast majority of Muskogees adopted the growing number of runaways who reached them in the 1760s." Blacks could become formally adopted and identified as fully Creeks, entitled to full benefits, when they put down roots in the Creek Nation, usually by marriage. Though among some Creeks there was antipathy to these newcomers, in general there was comity and ample room for these fellow marginalized people to find a home in Creek country.

Many Creek saw these people who helped till their land as their equals. They saw these Black people as kin, brothers and sisters, fully Creek and fully Black. But white people like Ethan Allen Hitchcock couldn't see or accept the beauty of this complex identity.

"Whites described these people [Black Creeks] as slaves, but they more closely resembled dependents," Saunt wrote. A white minister from Georgia observed that when the Muskogee tribe took captives after battle, they would kill the old white people and take "the young ones as slaves to their tribe where they receive the same treatment as the other Indians and in time marry into the Indian families."

But white supremacy has a way of creating divisions among marginalized groups that we marginalized folk never drew ourselves.

As the colonialists gained control of Florida, Cow Tom's birth state, they actively worried about Black people—slave, Freedmen, or never enslaved—further allying with the Creek. In fact, on September 26, 1767, John Stuart, then a seasoned forty-nine-year-old British superintendent of Indian affairs, wrote to Thomas Gage, the eventual commander in chief of the British armed forces during the Revolutionary War, on Indian relations. Stuart and his colonial peers worked actively to, as he put it, "prevent the Indian country

[from] becoming an asylum for negroes." For their capitalism to thrive, they needed an underclass of people who couldn't be part of this new land called the United States of America.

The problem of slavery in the United States, this sin, started with white men desperate to make a dime at a cheaper cost than ever before. And they feared that Blacks might make their home in a place "where slaves and masters could scarcely be distinguished." In the Creek Nation this was the case: Cow Tom and Yargee's only distinguishing factor was Cow Tom's black skin. That's why he was "Yargee's Negro."

Even if Cow Tom began life in the Creek Nation as a slave, he could become fully Creek. William Bartram, a naturalist and explorer who traveled extensively throughout the Cherokee and Creek Nations, noted that while on a Creek plantation the "slaves remained in servitude until they married Indians at which time they become Indians or Free Citizens." "Slave" was a misnomer not just because it didn't fully describe who Cow Tom and others were but also because it didn't accommodate for the fluid and dynamic nature of these terms in Creek life—it could never describe who Cow Tom and others *could be*.

When we give people names that they did not give themselves, we erase the identity they and their ancestors fought for. The labels we give them come preloaded with definitions limited by our imaginations. For Cow Tom, his "slave" label came with definitions of being *less than*. His label came preloaded with definitions of his descendants. Because if Cow Tom was a slave, then his children and children's children and all who came after would be children of slaves or slaves themselves. They could never access being free men and women who knew what it meant to be fully Creek and fully Black.

And if Cow Tom couldn't be both Creek and Black then, and they can't be Creek and Black now, then the battles they're fighting today to reclaim their families' history will be for naught.

BORN SOMETIME AROUND 1810 in what's now Florida, Cow Tom tended the cattle of Yargee along the western coast. According to Cow Tom's family, Cow Tom was probably part of the Yamasee, a multiethnic tribe in the southeastern United States. Though they would one day be subsumed into the Creek Nation, the Yamasee were known to be notably darker than the Creeks. The Yamasee lived under Spanish rule when the Spanish arrived in Florida around 1570. Having established a foothold in the Caribbean, the Spaniards began to subjugate the Yamasee into forced labor, which led to the intermixing of the southeastern Indians and people from the West Indies. Cow Tom's family's oral history indicates that this is where Cow Tom's fighting spirit comes from: the Yamasee, who fought hard against the introduction of forced labor by the Spanish during the 1680s and 1690s. Many fled to the English in South Carolina. But the many battles, trade disputes, and massacres in the area eventually drove the Yamasee back to Florida to settle near where Pensacola and St. Augustine are today, the region where, experts believe, Cow Tom was born. Growing up among the ever-mixing populations is what led to his language skills. These skills made him a "cultural broker," and the same could be said of many other Black Creeks.

Cow Tom's ability to communicate with white settlers became indispensable, and not just for Yargee. Straddling the land of the Creeks and the ever-encroaching land of violent white men, Cow

Tom also sold his interpretation skills (or, alternatively, was leased out by Yargee) to the army, which desperately needed interpreters.

THE SEMINOLE, though they skirmished numerous times with the Creek, can be considered kin of the Creek. They emerged during the eighteenth century as a subset of the Muskogee tribe, the progenitors of what we now consider the Creek Nation. Many rituals, such as the Green Corn Dance, and even one of three official languages came from the Creek and are now adopted by the Seminole. Like the Creek, the Seminole Nation received many freed Blacks, Blacks who had never been enslaved, and Blacks who were adopted or married into the tribe.

The Second Seminole War of 1835–1842 pitted numerous tribes against one another as they were moved by the U.S. government into an ever-shrinking land area and competed to determine who would have claim to it. This struggle also sparked the attention of the U.S. government, which had a stake in seeing that nearly every Native American move as far west as possible so that the land they once lived on could be settled by and sold to white men.

At that time, Major General Thomas Jesup had a knack for suppressing Native American resistance efforts, as he had done in the Creek War of 1836. In April of that year, Jesup was sent to deal with the Seminole and was assigned an interpreter: Cow Tom.

Because one of the official languages of the Seminole is Creek, and because Seminoles are related to the Creek, Cow Tom was the best choice to interpret for the very man whose desire it was to exterminate the Seminoles. While Cow Tom had served several

American military leaders, he was reassigned to Jesup, known today as the "Father of the Modern Quartermaster Corps." Cow Tom, like other Black interpreters, was often referred to by white soldiers as an "Indian-Negro." And though these interpreters were often not formally educated, they carried some of the most important information among regiments, soldiers, and leaders. "Interpreters . . . even though they were usually slaves," explained John Mahon in *History of the Second Seminole War 1835–1842*, "were as important in any negotiation as the most exalted person present."

WHEN THE UNITED STATES compelled Indian Nations to move west, Cow Tom went with Yargee in 1837. This was in part because Cow Tom, according to Jonathan Greenberg, the biographer of Jake Simmons Jr., one of Cow Tom's direct descendants, "had seen enough to know that whatever fate awaited his family in Indian Territory was preferable to the harsh bigotry of the white man's world." Moreover, Cow Tom realized that it would be to his advantage, and the advantage of many Blacks who lived among the Creeks, to move as far away as possible from Southern whites. As Greenberg wrote, "To Cow Tom the land of opportunity in 1837 was not America but a place beyond its reach: the land of the red and black."

Though many people perished on the Trail of Tears, the long march to the captivity of the unknown, Cow Tom's family survived the relocation. Their survival was nothing short of a miracle, especially compared with the devastation that relocation caused the Creek Nation. The Nation's population decreased as malaria and other diseases sapped their strength and ended lives. More than

24,000 Creeks left the southeastern United States during removal. Some thirty years later, right after the Civil War, in 1865—and even with new children born in the previous decades—only 13,500 were still living.

Somehow Cow Tom—and many of the Nation's other Black people—were not fated for death. In fact, while the Creek population continued to decline, its Black population nearly quadrupled.

Not long after settling in Indian Territory in what is now Oklahoma, Cow Tom put together approximately $400 to buy his outright freedom. Now fully his own man, Cow Tom could be paid without having to share it with Yargee. In fact, Cow Tom was able to pocket $2.50 per day for his services as an interpreter, nearly three times as much as a blacksmith's wages, and in today's dollars more than a full day's work at the federal minimum wage in America.

So Cow Tom started to do what, twenty years before, he told Hitchcock he hoped he'd do: he bought the freedom of his wife and daughters and bought land. And by 1861, on that land, he had "70 cows, 60 steers, 110 hogs, 11 yoke oxen, ten horses, and 500 bushels of corn." On his land, he installed a grist mill that allowed him to grind his cash crops. A school soon came where his children, grandchildren, and great-grandchildren would learn. And his citizenship was Creek, just like the estimated 1,600 free Black Creeks of the Nation of the time, though there were some 1,600 other Black people who were not free (though whether enslaved or simply intermarried, without yet applying for citizenship, is unclear). He prospered. He who had been simply "his Negro Tom" had become Cow Tom, a successful Black Creek. He shattered whatever expectations Hitchcock may have had for him.

. . .

THE UNITED STATES REACHED its fever pitch for the Creeks in 1863, during the height of the Civil War. At the time there were two clans in the Nation: Upper Creek and Lower Creek. Yargee—now Cow Tom's client, no longer his owner or boss—was the head of the Upper Creek. They had little interest in mixing with whites, but they readily embraced Blacks as fully Creek. Even being a former slave or having the title "Freedman" did not preclude someone from being fully Creek. Upper Creeks were often at odds with the Lower Creeks, who had a reputation for intermarrying with whites and more fully embracing the lower value that Southern white society placed on Black lives. The Lower Creeks made clear their disdain for Black Creeks by seeking to expel them from the tribe and by signing a treaty with the Confederacy during the Civil War to continue the enslavement of Blacks. White supremacy had found a home with the Lower Creeks.

One would think that Cow Tom, because he lived among the Upper Creeks along the Canadian River on the eastern side of Indian Territory, could've avoided becoming enmeshed in the Civil War. But the Battle of Honey Springs on July 17, 1863, changed all of that.

In the battle, Union soldiers vanquished the Confederates, which gave the Union control of Indian Territory. But the Lower Creeks affiliated with the Confederacy as well as several hundred surviving Confederate soldiers who ran from battle quickly encroached on Cow Tom's land. Luckily, Cow Tom escaped with his family, abandoning their home with only the clothes on their backs and enough provisions to make it to Fort Gibson, a Union outpost in Oklahoma, a week later. Suddenly, Cow Tom—like the many other Creeks gathering at the fort—was again a refugee. First from his home in Florida during Indian Removal, and now from the land he owned during the Civil War.

It was at Fort Gibson where the Creeks were brought to one of their lowest moments and Cow Tom's leadership would be tested most. Because of this battle, the largest on Indian Territory, the Nation was living in fractured chaos; some had escaped with Cow Tom to Fort Gibson, and another large portion of the Nation had escaped north all the way to Kansas, where sadly many would be stranded and die. This split allowed the Union to gain control of a major intersection of supply routes and traffic. While the hands of capitalism and commerce are supposedly invisible, the impact was visible: swatting Creek families apart. To make matters worse, especially for the Confederate soldiers, the day of the battle and many of the days around it were rainy, which ruined their gunpowder and waterlogged their already shoddy supplies. For the Creek, it meant traversing soggy patches, overrun creeks, and other bodies of water as they dispersed into the seemingly unknown for safety. There was no lamplight to ease their escape. No highways to shorten their travel. And few depots, miles from one another, as Cow Tom made his way with his family, often at night to avoid being spotted by soldiers, some twenty or so miles to Fort Gibson.

At fifty-three, Cow Tom took charge of the refugee Creeks. Able-bodied Creek men were conscripted by the Union; women, children, and older men were ordered to be put on dwindling rations. At times they were seen "tagging behind the mules of the military's supply caravans, scooping up bits of corn that fell to the ground," according to Commissioner of Indian Affairs Dennis Cooley's commission report in 1864.

Cow Tom saw what was happening and stepped in to stop the chaos and bring some sanity back to his people. He negotiated with Union military and government officials on behalf of the Creeks. Eventually, he directed a regiment of Black Creek soldiers who would protect Fort Gibson. He assumed leadership—it was not given—of the Creek Nation, which was now refugees surviving on threadbare resources. He and his comrade Harry Island organized the distribution of supplies and resources to the Creek as they came off wagon shipments. He acted as an interpreter for the Creeks, and he and Island became the de facto leaders. At the start of the Civil War, some of the Upper Creeks fled to Kansas. But by May 1864, the Union accompanied the five thousand Creek refugees from Kansas down to Fort Gibson. Flooded with the new arrivals, the small military outpost was taken over by a new Creek leader, Chief Sands, while Cow Tom shifted his leadership exclusively to the Black Creeks. Nevertheless, Cow Tom was still considered a chief, often called Micco.

Sands knew that it was time to negotiate with the United States, but he also knew he couldn't negotiate without Cow Tom (and Harry Island, now chief interpreter for the Creek Nation with the United States).

With Civil War battles; the loss of nearly three hundred thousand cattle; the leveling of homes; the rise of disease, famine, and malnutrition; and the continued warring within the Nation itself (mainly Lower vs. Upper Creeks), nearly 25 percent of the Creek Nation would die by 1867. The Lower Creek—like their allies, the white Southerners—were scattered and diminished. And as with white Southerners, their racism and white supremacy stayed intact even after the Civil War ended.

To make matters worse, the United States punished the entire

Creek Nation for the Lower Creeks' decision to side with the Confederacy and took full advantage of a Nation in survival mode. Federal law dictated that if any tribe signed a treaty with the Confederates, any preexisting treaty became void. This new regulation freed up land for the U.S. government to reallocate to the rising railroad interests, which quickly ran through Creek claims to land.

These incursions on Creek sovereignty spelled doom for the Creek Nation. On the other hand, these incursions created opportunities for Black Creeks to, as Imani Perry, professor of African American studies at Princeton, wrote, "keep making generations to collect our inheritance."

In September 1865, just months after the Civil War ended, leaders of the Five Nations made their way to Fort Smith, Arkansas, to negotiate peace treaties. Cow Tom and Harry Island, along with three other Black Creek delegates, were the only Black people at this first round of negotiations. But this early statement of diversity did not come without consequences.

The Lower Creeks, like white Southerners, were angry at the federal government as the government forced them to assign more value to Blacks than they were ready to commit. Most vocal among these racist Lower Creeks was Samuel Checote. He was an admirer of how the states of the former Confederacy had after the war immediately implemented "Black Codes" that limited the freedom of Blacks. (This was during Reconstruction, when President Andrew Johnson left the fate of Southern Blacks to state governments.)

Checote wanted Black Codes in the Creek Nation. In fact, he knew then that with Blacks representing nearly 17 percent of the Creek Nation, granting Blacks citizenship rights would also grant them access to tribal funds. If Cow Tom and his Black counterparts in the Creek Nation became citizens, people like Checote assumed that their disbursements from the U.S. government would decrease by more than 15 percent. This faction's racism cloaked in economic preservation caused Cow Tom and Harry Island to push seriously not only for a guarantee of freedom, but for complete Black enfranchisement within the Nation.

At the peace conference, Harry Island read a statement on behalf of the Upper Creeks that articulated this fervor for freedom for Black Creeks, which said in part: "We are willing to provide for the abolishing of slavery and settlement of the Blacks who were among us at the breaking out of the rebellion, as slaves or otherwise as citizens entitled to all the rights and privileges that we are."

By the beginning of 1866, these negotiations had become a matter of such interest that they landed on the desk of secretary of the interior James Harlan, and new negotiations were convened first in Fort Smith— a spoil of the Union's defeat of the Confederate Army that sprang Cow Tom into leadership of the Nation—and then finally in Washington, D.C., by perhaps the most subtle of American power players, Dennis Cooley, the "Convener-in-Chief." Without these two men, the Black Creek cause would have been hollowed out before their effort hit any sort of stride, even if to some extent the Black Creek cause advanced while the general Creek claim to its land and autonomy shrank even further.

NELSON A. MILES, the former commanding general of the U.S. Army, once said that "our relations with the Indians have been governed chiefly by treaties and trade, or war and subjugation." What Miles did not realize was that treaties with Indigenous counterparts beget trade, and that disagreements on trade often beget war, and the results of war are all too often subjugation of the vanquished. And subjugation often was the United States' preferred position before subjugation got delayed by treaties, trade, and wars. The treaties between the United States and the Five Tribes were negotiated with the same force and power dynamics that an army with more troops and more guns that steps onto a battlefield has, assured of victory and unconcerned with preserving the interests of the people they are bound to beat.

As leader of these negotiations Cooley remains a little-known figure in Civil War history. To Cow Tom, he would have been as important as any U.S. president.

Though born in New Hampshire in 1825, Dennis Cooley was an Iowan through and through. He charted his own course in life at age fifteen, when he left home for seminary and then college, graduating with a law degree. As Cooley established himself as a lawyer in Iowa, he became a critical fixture in Republican politics. Cooley was rewarded for his loyalty to the party by Abraham Lincoln, who made him the commissioner of South Carolina, representing the interests of the federal government in Washington, D.C., in a state that was teetering on secession. Within short order, Lincoln doubled Cooley's responsibility—appointing him special commissioner, tasked with settling deeds, titles, and land rights in the state, which also made him the quasi tax commissioner for the city of Charleston. During some of America's most calamitous times, Cooley tried to bring as much stability as he could in this shaky Southern state.

Once the Civil War ended, Cooley's dynamism as a leader, his expertise in maintaining calm even in wartime, and his mastery of land and property rights made him the obvious pick as commissioner of Indian affairs for President Andrew Johnson. The federal government at the time was desperate to consolidate and centralize power. Much Indian land had been fought on, in some cases deserted, and in many cases squandered and misused by Union and Confederate troops. Some Nations, like the Choctaw and the Chickasaw, which by and large had sided with the Confederacy, were bigger targets for punishment, while the Creeks, who mainly sided with the Union, were due to be spared more, along with the Cherokee and Seminole Nations. Implementing such punishments and sparing was left to Cooley.

And implement Cooley did, knowing that beyond the Union victory and Confederate defeat, there were Nations whose land had seen battles and whose men were conscripted into both sides of the war effort. The negotiations he convened to bolster his bona fides were both savvy and brutal.

Peter Pitchlynn, the principal chief of the Choctaw Republic, who surrendered to the United States on behalf of the Choctaw at the end of the Civil War, had been on the receiving end of this bullying. He testified in 1872 before the U.S. House of Representatives Subcommittee on Indian Affairs.

Pitchlynn told the committee that he hadn't been asked to be at the initial treaty negotiations because the first negotiators weren't as deft as Cooley. They discounted the value of Pitchlynn's perspective as a Choctaw. Cooley knew that speaking with the Choctaw themselves might make them adhere to the treaty's terms more than allowing white men to represent the Choctaws' interests to the U.S. government. Pitchlynn said as much when he told the subcommittee, "I was sent for by Mr. Cooley for the United States."

Cooley likely knew that for a Nation to accept the terms of a deal

imposed by their oppressors, the Choctaw would be better off striking a deal directly with the people who were offering the terms. As
Pitchlynn admitted, "Mr. Cooley told me himself that he and I could
have sat down and made a better treaty than they [the Choctaw ne-
gotiators] made with the United States. That was a complimentary
way of talking to me."

Another Choctaw leader, Allen Wright, attested to Cooley's sav-
viness. Wright felt that the Choctaw citizens were getting the short
end of the stick when they were paying for land surveys that would
cause them to lose more land. He lodged a complaint with Cooley
while in Washington. Cooley, in turn, made the power dynamics
clear, telling him, "You must not raise the question of right here. Do
you see that white house upon the hill?" He pointed to the Capitol.
"It is not a question of right, but a question of might."

This may sound like bullying, but it was the bullying that brought
the Creek to the negotiating table in 1866 to determine, among other
matters, just how much dignity and equality Black Creeks like Cow
Tom and others would have in post–Civil War America.

CHAPTER 5

THE MORAL MAN

Senator Harlan is a good man.

PRESIDENT ABRAHAM LINCOLN

On January 24, 1865, the poet Walt Whitman started a new job at the Bureau of Indian Affairs in the Department of the Interior, where he served as clerk, making a grand sum of $1,200 per year (about $18,875 today). Within four short months, Whitman got a promotion to a more senior clerkship in the Interior Department.

Yet Whitman's run of luck was brief: his job was about to meet a swift end thanks to a streak of morality.

The new secretary of the interior, James Harlan, appointed by Andrew Johnson after the assassination of Abraham Lincoln in April, came on a mission to "clean house," promising to fire "a considerable number of incumbents who were seldom at their respective desks." Harlan had been such good friends with Lincoln that he recalled long carriage rides with Lincoln and his wife. "During these drives to the country we had, of course, unrestrained conversation with each other—very much, I think, as if we had been members of the same family." His devotion to Lincoln and to his own moral compass made even written acceptance of the nomination to serve as secretary of the interior confusing. "If the position of Secretary of the Interior should be formally tendered to me by the President," Harlan once wrote, "I would then consider seriously the question of my duty in the premises." One would consider a simple yes sufficient, but perhaps the combination of the lofty office, the dangerous time the country was going through, and his deliberative style compelled Harlan to use more words when fewer would be better. "If I should conclude that I would be more useful to my country in that position, than in the one I now hold, I would resign the latter and accept the former; but I would not, I think, permit personal considerations to influence me in the least." In short, "I accept this position, but I want you to know that this is a decision born of selflessness, sacrifice, and moral obligation."

It appeared that Whitman didn't meet Harlan's order of morality—the type of morality Harlan represented as the "propriety proscribed by a Christian Civilization."

The month that Whitman got his promotion was the same month that Harlan ordered a detailed report of department employees who demonstrated undesirable behaviors, including the following:

1. Those who had uttered disloyal statements since the bombardment of Fort Sumter, which as we learned was the formal kickoff to the Civil War

2. All those not known to entertain loyal sentiments or who
   had associated with those known to be disloyal

3. Those who were inefficient or not necessary to transact
   public business

4. All such persons "as disregard in their conduct, habits and
   associations, the rules of decorum [and] propriety proscribed by a Christian Civilization"

Whitman had five years earlier published the now-classic *Leaves of Grass*, and a copy of it sat on Harlan's desk in Washington. The book was considered immoral by Harlan along with many other contemporaries. So Harlan did, out of some high-minded sense of duty, what no literary enthusiast would ever imagine allowable: he fired Whitman.

Strict adherence to standards was typical for Harlan. But his reverence for a correct morality knew no bounds, and his adherence to such views may have been the greatest aid to the Black Creek cause.

HARLAN, THOUGH BORN in Illinois and raised in Indiana and a graduate of what is now DePauw University, made his way to Iowa City at twenty-five and soon found his calling in public service. He became superintendent of Iowa City's burgeoning school system while simultaneously studying law and passing the Iowa bar. Immediately after finishing his law studies in 1850, he was offered but then declined a nomination for governor of the state he had arrived in only five years earlier. As for others of this time, leadership happened fast and young. So it isn't that surprising that by age thirty-three, Harlan became president of a local college.

Before the Seventeenth Amendment was ratified in 1913, U.S. senators were chosen by each state's legislatures. The posts were usually given to men of repute and distinction within each state. After an electoral snafu, the Iowa legislature fully vested Harlan as a senator in 1857. It was while he was a senator that his relationship with Lincoln grew, leading to Harlan's serving as a delegate to the 1861 peace conference in Virginia that tried to prevent the Civil War.

It was perhaps at the conference of Virginia that the fates of Cow Tom and the Black Creek were sealed—long before they knew what was to come.

IT WAS FEBRUARY 1861. Lincoln was about to be inaugurated as president. Partisanship and intransigence had grown along the lines of slavery, which for decades had been the financial lifeblood of the South. The past two presidents, James Buchanan and Franklin Pierce, though Northerners, had strong sympathies for Southern Democrats who wanted to preserve the institution of slavery. By this point, many Southern states had sent delegates to special conventions to discuss seceding, resulting in seven states leaving the Union by early 1861. Congress had tried and failed to reach compromise in the House of Representatives to prevent the full secession of the rest of the South.

The failures racked up as the Union and the burgeoning Confederacy couldn't come to a compromise. It was in Virginia that former president John Tyler, then a private citizen, was enlisted to reconvene the disagreeing parties to try to reach a compromise. The Civil War began in earnest not long after, making this the fourth and final attempt to prevent war.

The breakdown in talks was due in part to Senator James Harlan.

While Harlan didn't want to necessarily undo states' rights, as John Calhoun had long alleged the North wanted to do, Harlan would not budge on slavery: it was immoral. In fact, members of the Southern delegation at the Virginia conference tried to convince Harlan to "embrace a proposal designed to ensure that any anti-slavery legislation could always be vetoed." Harlan refused and announced that he would oppose any proposal that would reverse anti-slavery legislation. Because Harlan and other Republicans refused to shelve the South's recommendations for curtailing the anti-slavery movement, they became more reluctant to accommodate any of the South's demands to retain slavery. And it didn't stop there. Harlan became one of two at the convention who voted against an amendment that would ensure that the federal government would never interfere in the operations of states where slavery existed.

Harlan was disposed to do away with the very institution that propped up the significant economic gains of America. It was this moral stance that paved the way for the Black Creek to come under the purview of Harlan's decision making. And it wouldn't end well.

IN 1865, Harlan wrote in *The New York Times*: "If I should be in Iowa when [negro suffrage] is submitted to the people, if it shall be so submitted by the Legislature, I would vote to extend the right to all classes of persons possessing the requisite intelligence and patriotism to be intrusted with a participation in the management of public affairs, State or national, without regard to their nationality, as I do not believe that the liberty of any class of people can be considered safe who are to be permanently deprived of the exercise of this right."

Five months before Harlan wrote this, Lincoln had been assassinated. Soon after, Harlan resigned his Senate seat to accept the nomination by President Andrew Johnson as secretary of the interior. The Civil War had come to its close, but the true impact of the war had only begun to be known.

If your high school U.S. history teacher was anything like mine—a Southern sympathizer who called the Civil War the War of Northern Aggression and who thought that slavery was a matter of states' rights, never worth a war—you likely learned few details about the Civil War, and details about what happened after the war was over were certainly glossed over.

The United States was far from united after the Civil War. In fact, it was arguably just as divided, except this time the Southern economy was in ruins, the North's economy wasn't in much better shape, and Indian Territory was compromised.

Nearly eight thousand Native Americans participated in the Civil War, most of whom were conscripted by one side or the other (the rest were part of diplomatic and political concerns, taking bets on who would emerge the winner).

Hundreds of Native Americans died in this battle. By the end of 1863, more than four thousand Creek and Cherokee had died—some fighting for the South and others for the North. These split loyalties did not inspire any love of the Union.

With thousands dead, economies drained, and a federal government desperate to reconsolidate power and authority, Harlan's largest moral stand was set to take root.

Suffrage and liberation from slavery were causes Harlan was determined to uphold. He and others like Dennis Cooley were committed to ensuring that those who sided with the Confederacy would pay for it.

Created by Congress, the Southern Treaty Commission was deputized to craft and negotiate treaties with the Indian Nations that had sided with the Confederacy. Cooley communicated with the leaders of all of the Five Nations that had sided with the Confederacy and told them that their old treaties were void and needed to be rewritten.

And in each of those treaties, Harlan's rigid point of view on slavery became clear, as the opportunities for Cow Tom and the Black Creek cause aligned with the goal of emancipation. This commission set the stage for the treaty that Cow Tom would sign on behalf of the Creek.

HARLAN'S DEVOTION to his convictions eventually found him on the outs with perhaps the most unpopular president in American history up to that time: Andrew Johnson. Johnson was under fire from Radical Republicans and moderates like Harlan for many reasons, perhaps most for Johnson's laissez-faire attitude toward the South's transition out of slavery. It was Harlan who wrote that if there was a chance to vote for negro suffrage, he would. So you can imagine that Johnson's penchant for "conciliation and forgiveness toward the Southerners who had led the Confederacy" damaged what little support he had from these Republicans.

Johnson's opponents wanted to enact laws that ensured the same rights for recently freed Blacks as for whites, codify the economic and political opportunities for slaves, and install federal military outposts in the South to guarantee the safety of Black suffrage. Harlan and others felt that giving Southern states the opportunity to slowly craft the means of their own reconstruction and reaffirm their individual rights would limit opportunities for Black people. This was exactly what happened. Black Codes arose in states across the South to limit and restrict the lives and livelihoods of Black citizens.

Johnson's feckless leadership on the issue of Black life in America caused Harlan to resign from Johnson's cabinet, and he was returned to the Senate to join the other members of Iowa's congressional delegation to push for Reconstruction in the South that would truly reconstitute opportunities for Black families. On July 30, 1866, *The Daily Ohio Statesman* wrote, "It will delight the Conservatives of the country to learn that the Hon. James Harlan has resigned as Secretary of the Interior." These conservatives were delighted because they understood that an enemy of Black subjugation in the South had left the cabinet.

Cow Tom, Harry Island, and the other Creek Nation delegates went to Washington, D.C., to try to strike a deal, but it might not have included the extension of rights Blacks once received had Dennis Cooley not been Convener-in-Chief and had James Harlan not been, as Lincoln had called him, a "good man."

CHAPTER 6

THE GIFT HE GAVE

But freedom was also to be found in the
West of the old Indian Territory.

RALPH ELLISON, *GOING TO THE TERRITORY*

After the Civil War, the Upper Creeks were summoned by Harlan in 1866 to finalize the peace treaty between the U.S. government and the Creek Nation. Once Samuel Checote received word of these impending negotiations, he put his political machine to work, trying to undo whatever racial progress there was to be made. He argued that the treaty would not be valid until it was agreed to by both Upper and Lower Creeks.

The Lower Creeks managed to forestall negotiations by six months, exhausting federal government leaders who just wanted a signed treaty. The sticking point for the Lower Creeks was accepting the adoption of Blacks as full members of the Creek Nation. This they refused to agree to. The federal government, realizing that the impasse was calcifying, leaned on Chief Sands of the Upper Creeks to compromise on enfranchising Blacks. But Harry Island and Cow Tom, now senior advisers to Sands, wouldn't relent: free Black Creeks would continue to be full members of the Nation.

Dennis Cooley, then Indian Affairs commissioner, recounted how the interests of Harry Island and Cow Tom prevailed:

> They were disposed to urge the national delegates to yield the point [the Black Creek enfranchisement] for the present, but they held out firmly for the freedmen, urging that . . . they promised their slaves that if they would also remain faithful to the government, they should be free as themselves. Under these circumstances the delegates refused to yield, but insisted that that sacred pledge should be fulfilled, declaring that they would sooner go home and fight and suffer again with their faithful friends [Black Creeks] than abandon the point [their enfranchisement]. They were successful at last, and the treaty guaranteed to their freedmen full equality.

With the signing of this treaty in 1866, the future of Black Creeks was sealed for perpetuity.

Or so they thought.

Etched into the treaty was a new fate for the Black Creek, which Hitchcock could not have foreseen when he met "his Negro Tom." Black Creeks have Cow Tom to thank for their inherited freedom, citizenship, and—as we will soon learn—the prosperity this citizenship and freedom would provide.

Even at the time people knew that it was Cow Tom who had won equality for his people. An unnamed Native American source in the early 1870s put it crudely but accurately when he wrote, "The reason the niggers got equalization [in the Creek Nation] was because they had a nigger interpreter who looked out for his own people." But in Cow Tom's looking out for his own people and despite the growth in opportunity for Black Creeks, the treaty itself also forced further cessions of land. This, as Dr. Alaina Roberts wrote in her book *I've Been Here All the While*, made "Indian freedpeople . . . the only people of African descent in the world to receive what might be viewed as reparations for their enslavement on a large scale."

So, with negotiations completed, Cow Tom returned to his wife, Amy, and his land along the Canadian River, where a federal agent noted in 1866 that Blacks "are today further from want than are their former masters." As he worked his land, growing corn and raising cattle, Cow Tom tried to stay out of politics. But he found himself making a brief reentry onto the political scene.

As president, Johnson was no advocate of granting federally guaranteed rights to African Americans. In fact, he spent his time in office sympathizing with racist sentiments woven into calls for states' rights. By then, James Harlan had resigned as secretary of the interior. And Dennis Cooley had been replaced as Indian Affairs commissioner by Lewis Bogy, who didn't care much for the Black Creek cause. The defenders of that treaty were gone.

It was March 14, 1867, and all Creeks, regardless of race, were set to receive their $17.34 worth of gold in per capita allotments, roughly the earnings from an entire season's crop. But before that gold could reach Black hands, a messenger from Washington arrived to remove the Black Freedmen from the Creek Nation census. Confederate Creeks with racist sympathies had nixed Blacks from the census, which dashed their hopes of getting federal disbursements, even though Blacks had representation in the House of Lords and House of Warriors, the bicameral governing body for the Creek Nation.

Cow Tom and Harry Island believed that this census removal would be the first shove down a slippery slope. If Black Freedmen were removed from the census, what other resources of the Black Creek would be lost? So the two returned to the political fray.

To remove Black Creeks from the census, Checote had appealed to an Indian affairs commissioner in Washington, D.C., going above the head of the federal agent assigned to conduct censuses and disbursements for the Creek Nation. The commissioner agreed to the excision. So Cow Tom and Harry Island went above the head of the commission, and above the secretary of the interior, Orville Browning, right to Congress.

They approached Congress at precisely the right time. Johnson had been impeached by the House and avoided a Senate conviction by just one vote, and the Radical Republicans had earned a veto-proof majority, passing legislation to advance rights for Blacks. Cow Tom and Island worked with Samuel Pomeroy, a U.S. senator from Kansas, who introduced a resolution on the Senate floor demanding that Browning explain why Black Creeks had been removed from the Creek Nation census rolls, therefore denying per capita allotment. When it passed, Browning told the Senate that Blacks weren't entitled to be listed on that census nor to any government funds. In essence, the secretary of the interior ignored a treaty that had been approved by the very Senate that had asked for an explanation— proving that atoning for America's original sin didn't end with a civil war.

The Radical Republicans in the Senate compelled Browning to

follow the law. Which Browning did: the Black Creeks received their disbursement. The tenets of the treaty remained in effect until 1979, when Cow Tom's Blackness injured his descendants' claim to their Creek heritage.

COW TOM DIED on June 1, 1874, and he was buried in a small plot not far from where he had built his home. Two years before he died, his extraordinary exploits were writ on congressional testimony. "My name is Cow mikko," he told a House committee. Which means that he wasn't just a member, he was a leader of the Creek Nation. And when they asked him about what he did for a living and whether he held any office in the Creek Nation, he told them, "[I] am a farmer and stock-raiser. . . . At the present time I am on the supreme bench of the nation. I was a delegate to Washington to make the treaty of 1866." Great though he was, the legacy he left would stand longer than even the memory of his existence.

His small plot in Muskogee County, Oklahoma, sits next to that of his wife, who died two years after he did. He left land that would sustain his family through a depression, that would raise cattle that would make his grandchildren wealthy, and that would run rich with oil. He left his family with boots equipped with straps that most Black people are chastised for not pulling themselves up by. His kids got the leg up that kids need to make it in America. But more important than any one opportunity, Cow Tom left for his family an identity, a sacred certainty of who they are so that they could forever define themselves apart from what white people—or any people— had to say about it.

CHAPTER 7

. . . AND OKLAHOMA BECAME THE SOUTH

Dispersed from their countries of origin and perpetually
homeless on this continent, African Americans have
imagined into being a Promised Land that is located both
within and outside the national boundaries of the United
States. In the realm of the black imaginary, then, the site of
the Indian has been present, persistent, and paramount.

TIYA MILES AND SHARON P. HOLLAND,
CROSSING WATERS, CROSSING WORLDS

As exceptional as what happened to Cow Tom was, it's even
more exceptional to learn that one of his relatives, another
Black Creek man, would lead the Creek Nation years later
and help found the town in which I grew up.

When I was seven years old, my family moved to Oklahoma from

New York City. We moved to South Tulsa, which is what my grand-father would call "Pilgrim"—in other words, incredibly white. The private Christian schools my Jamaican parents put me in were even whiter, if that is possible.

Tulsa can be cut five ways: North Tulsa, South Tulsa, East Tulsa, West Tulsa, and Midtown Tulsa. All of those parts except North Tulsa looked just as white as my school, or at least that's what I thought. We'd go to church, though, in North Tulsa. And in those churches, we'd find the very Black people we wanted to be around. My mother called them "saved, sanctified folk."

As a teenager, I had all but given up trying to learn about Black Tulsa. But that changed one Sunday in 2006. My father and I, to make extra money, had a large paper route where we delivered the *Tulsa World* in white neighborhoods. So I had my hand on the pulse of the news—at least Tulsa news and usually before the news was widely circulated. That day a headline on the front page caught my eye: "'We Don't Deliver': Tulsa's Northside Left Out."

According to the piece, Mark White, an owner of ten Domino's Pizza franchises in the Tulsa area, had essentially declared that he would not deliver pizzas to North Tulsa. The article quoted Sharisa McClennan, a North Tulsa resident who for years couldn't get a Domino's pizza delivered to her house. When she tried, she always got the same answer. "They say it's out of their service area," said McClennan. "You can't make anyone offer a service, but it has a bad suggestive undertone."

What White did not know at the time was that the fear he had of North Tulsa in 2006 was directly tied to the racism in Tulsa from a century before. Perhaps if he knew this history—and that of Legus

Perryman—he would think differently about North Tulsa and the people who lived there.

The Perrymans, perhaps the most racially and ethnically complex family in Oklahoma history, helped to found Tulsa, once called Tulsey Town. And a man whose status was both fully Black and fully Creek, Legus Perryman, once saw Tulsa far differently from how we see it today.

No Oklahoma history class taught me about a Tulsa whose founders included a family, some of whom were white, some of whom were mixed (white and Creek, Creek and Black, white and Black), some of whom were slaveholders, and others who missed enslavement because of the traditions and legacies of the Creek. I didn't know that Legus Perryman was related to Cow Tom. I didn't know that the city's first post office was founded by a Black man: Legus's brother, Josiah. I couldn't imagine a Tulsa through the lens that they likely viewed it through: living on land owned by them by virtue of their Indigenous ancestry.

Tulsa is a place whose legacy never quite leaves the city alone. Its history haunts it. It's been the setting for some of the more confusing episodes of racial violence in America. Black life in Tulsa was never simple, and certainly not as simple as we'd like it to be. The story of Cow Tom and his descendants in Tulsa invites you to figure out how your history can and will forever enable you to become. And perhaps most important, this city, Tulsa, and this state, Oklahoma, have been, at times, bastions for experimenting with innovative approaches for how to belong. But the story of Legus Perryman, a darker-skinned

Black chief of the Creek Nation, elected twice, is the story of how Oklahoma became that much more racist. And it was that racism that upended the hopes for a unique form of racial progress.

THE OKLAHOMA CITY LAW OFFICES of Riggs, Abney, Neal, Turpen, Orbison & Lewis called to tell me that Sharon Lenzy-Scott was ready to talk with me about her case at seven p.m. the next day. She was suing the Creek Nation and the U.S. Department of the Interior for kicking her out of the Nation in 1979.

I left Tulsa at ten a.m. for a seven p.m. meeting that was a little more than a hundred miles away. Yet somehow, I found myself racing at the last minute to get there less than five minutes late. Why?

On my way to Oklahoma City, I decided to take a detour. Instead of driving southwest, I drove southeast toward Haskell, Red Bird, and a collection of other small towns you've never heard of. I went to Porter, population 566, which is known for its annual Peach Festival. I drove to Muskogee, Okmulgee, and (when I finally got close to Oklahoma City) Spencer, Boley, and Slick. These were all-Black towns that harbored the histories of people like Cow Tom and Legus Perryman.

In them I got lost, not geographically but historically.

Red Bird is forty-five minutes away from where I grew up. In her book *Crossing Waters, Crossing Worlds: The African Diaspora in Indian Country*, Tiya Miles talks about a brochure from the Red Bird Investment Company—owned and operated by Black people who were awarded land from Indian allotments—which read: "A Message to the Colored man . . . Do you want a home in the Great

Southwest—the Beautiful Indian Territory? In a town populated by intelligent, self-reliant colored people?"

Early in the twentieth century, Jason Mayer Conner, a minister in the African Methodist Episcopal Church, attested to this when he wrote, "I have made a personal visit to the Indian Territory and know it to be the best place on earth for the Negro." Others said of this territory that "this country is the Paradise for the colored people." A 1904 article in the *Muskogee Comet*, a Black newspaper, said of this area that it "may verily be called the Eden of the West for the colored people." Another Black newspaper, in Kansas, the *Afro-American Advocate*, sounded the clarion call to Black people across the South to "come home, come home . . . Come out of the wilderness from among these lawless lynchers and breathe the free air."

The Oklahoma that the Perrymans knew was quite different from the Oklahoma I knew. For most of their lives, Oklahoma wasn't Oklahoma—it was Indian Territory. The Perrymans were part of the Black bourgeoisie precisely because they were in Oklahoma. The part of Tulsa that Blacks settled, Booker T. Washington called "Negro Wall Street." W. E. B. Du Bois wrote of this Negro Wall Street: "I have never seen a colored community so highly organized as that of Tulsa. The colored people of Tulsa have accumulated property, have established stores and business organizations, and have made money in oil." And despite Mark White's twenty-first-century perspective on North Tulsa, it was said in the early twentieth century that this area "was so economically self-sufficient that purportedly a dollar circulated within the community fifty times, sometimes taking a year for currency to leave the community."

The Perrymans were part of this "Eden of the West for colored people" and were free from "these lawless lynchers"; here they could "breathe the free air." In other ways, the Oklahoma that Legus Perryman knew was similar to the one I knew, equipped with every level of race-based vitriol one could imagine. And the sin of white supremacy that begat America's original sin found its way into Oklahoma, what was once the Eden of the West for colored people.

WHEN I FINALLY ARRIVED in Oklahoma City, I met Sharon. I guessed that she stood no more than five feet, six inches, but she'd be much taller if she stood on the thousands of pages she submitted to the Bureau of Indian Affairs to recognize what she's known all of her life: that Creek identity and tribe leadership run in the family.

Sharon came to learn about being Creek, she told me, "from my mother, Adlene Perryman-Lenzy. Because then, in 1968, I remember them—receiving checks from the Creek Nation." Back then, the Creek Nation provided payments to its members based on revenue generated from what was owed to the Creek Nation: land deals and earnings through other activities. The treaties, though they limited what stake the Creek Nation overall could claim, determined who was Creek and subsequently who qualified for these payments. Today, the Muskogee (Creek) Nation does not distribute per capita payments; instead the Nation uses the funds it's paid for social services and health care for citizens. In fact, significant casino revenues are redistributed to education, social services, and health care assistance.

"But then it stopped," Sharon said.

"My mother . . . she had two sisters. They wondered why the

checks stopped. And, of course, they called the Creek Nation and they [were told] they were Freedmen and they weren't entitled to the money. And of course everything's based on the roll number. And they were considered Freedmen . . . on the Freedman roll." Being a Black Freedman or being "full-blood" Creek didn't matter to the Creek nearly as much as it mattered to the U.S. government, which came up with these distinctions more than a century ago. Sharon's mother and aunt "wrote to the Bureau of Indian Affairs [BIA] for them to find out as to what was going on actually getting them citizenship."

Adlene, Sharon, and the rest of their family were left to do what Black people have been doing for as long as Black people have been in America: trying to make a home in a place whose welcome was never warm and whose initial invite was no invite at all.

Belonging to the Creek Nation mattered so much to Sharon that in the early 2000s she started the painstaking process of appealing again for the Creek Nation to recognize not just her but her family's contribution to the Nation.

HEARING SHARON'S STORY and reading about the political success of Legus Perryman a hundred years before reveal a painful truth: as the Indian Territory entered the twentieth century, as it became Oklahoma, it became more blatantly racist, and the Creek Nation wasn't immune to that. In fact, the very treaty that assured people like Cow Tom and his descendants a home in the Creek Nation, Sharon included, also decreased its tribal authority of the Nation, which had the effect of legally marginalizing the Nation's Black citizen. Perhaps the most salient example of this could be found in the August 6, 1903, edition of the *South McAlester Capital*, which said of Legus, "Old Legus Perryman was sweating like a nigger."

And outside the Creek Nation, Oklahoma was doubling down on bolstering its anti-Black bona fides as it entered the Union in the early twentieth century. On December 18, 1907, Senate Bill One was passed by the state senate and signed by Charles N. Haskell, the first governor of Oklahoma. A month and two days before Senate Bill One was signed into law, Oklahoma was officially admitted to the Union. The Abbeville, South Carolina, *Press and Banner* ran a piece announcing the news:

> With impressive ceremonies befitting the birth of the new state of Oklahoma, the oaths of office were administered to Governor Charles N. Haskell and other state officers a few minutes before noon. . . . In one of the carriages were the chiefs of the five civilized tribes dressed as citizens. . . . Indians and whites mingled in picturesque good fellowship. Some of the Indians wore blankets and some squaws carried papooses. At the Carnegie Library [in Guthrie, Oklahoma] there was an allegorical marriage ceremony which joined Oklahoma and Indian Territory for life. C.G. Joines, of Oklahoma City, for many years one of the most tireless champions of joint statehood, was the bridegroom. He made the proposal of marriage to the bride, Miss Indian Territory, who was Mrs. Leo Bennett, of Muskogee, a beautiful native of the Cherokee Nation and wife of Dr. Leo Bennett.

The awkwardness of this report is obvious today. White men who settled the land, then took away Creek control over the land

they promised would be for Indigenous people only, were then cele-
brated for making this sacred territory their land — without permission. That is not just awkward, it is another promise broken. And
instead of lamenting the breaking of the promise, observers called
this a wedding, between these Indian Nations and this new state and
the United States of America.

Do you notice who was missing?

There's a simple reason Black lives are omitted from American
history: the presence of Black lives in our history always indicts
white America for generating prosperity on the backs of its own
people. Black existence and success shatter the illusion that Americans are exceptional and that our ascent has been attained without
keeping some of us down. And for that matter, the presence of Indian Nations indicts America just as much. So, of course, it had to
be a wedding—to convey that the relations between Indian Nations
and this new state in the Union were normalized. To be clear, things
were not normal.

In Oklahoma, it started with Senate Bill One, signed into law one
week after this metaphorical marriage between Indian Territory and
the State of Oklahoma arranged by the will and ambition of white
supremacy.

As the first two governors of Oklahoma, Charles Haskell
and Lee Cruce were politicians who knew that explicitly excluding
Blacks from the political process would scuttle any chance of admit-
ting Oklahoma as a state. Theodore Roosevelt was in the White
House, and he was keeping a watchful eye on Haskell and his actions toward Blacks. Roosevelt, a Republican and a progressive, was

the same president who had invited Booker T. Washington to dinner at the White House, an event that led to the infamous poem "Niggers in the White House" that was circulated around the country. As a result, Haskell and Cruce kept their plans to doom Black life in Oklahoma after it became a state.

Senate Bill One was colloquially called the "coach law" and brought the scourge of Jim Crow formally within Indian Territory's borders. It was passed 95–10. The bill ensured that "every railway company, urban or suburban car company, street car or interurban car or railway company" would provide "separate coaches or compartments as hereinafter provided for the accommodation of the white and negro races, which separate coaches or cars shall be equal in all points of comfort and convenience."

Following that section was one that mandated that each railroad depot must have "separate, adequately signed waiting rooms for each race." If a depot didn't do this, the railroad company and depot manager could face a fine of up to $1,000 (about $28,000 today). And if passengers didn't listen to a conductor when they were in the "wrong" coach or compartment, they would have to pay $25 (about $700 today). To soften the blow, the fines generated by the bill were earmarked for the state's "common school fund," because who doesn't want dollars earned through racist means to go to white children?

This bill was considered an emergency measure, which is why Senator H. E. P. Stanford abstained, refusing to vote because he didn't like that it was passed through the Senate as an emergency bill. Though not racially progressive, Stanford made it clear that he firmly stood with the law, clarifying that he had a problem with Black nurses and attendants even entering white coaches. When the bill got to the House, only the Republicans still drenched in the Civil War sentiment of anti-slavery voted against it.

I wondered how someone like Legus Perryman could go, over the course of his life, from being chief of a nation to being remembered, as the famed Creek poet and journalist Alex Posey called him, as "a nigger and a bad one at that." Posey aimed to stain Legus Perryman's reputation by maligning his Blackness. Blackness, or any racial identity isn't inherently bent on being good or bad. Black identity becomes dangerous when a Posey—or anyone else, for that matter—decides that being Black is inherently dangerous.

For a man as accomplished as Legus to be reduced to that description is another example of how white supremacy holds unfettered sway in America. Legus had to be a nigger, because it makes elevating white lives easier when there are Black and Brown lives to be stepped on.

ANGIE DEBO DESCRIBED the Perryman family and also spoke to the family's curious admixture of Black and non-Black ancestry when she wrote: "The ablest and most prominent mixed-blood family in the nation had received a noticeable strain of negro blood in its early history. The members of this family ignored this admixture without attempting to deny it and associated themselves with white-and-Indian Creeks; and so great was the respect felt for their character and ability that they were freely accepted even by this proud and aristocratic group. But except for this one numerous family the negro Indian admixture was confined to the full-bloods."

The Perryman family may confuse people. Legus was the nephew of Mose Perryman. Mose Perryman was one of eight children of

Benjamin Perryman, who migrated to the area during the Trail of Tears and was one of the earliest settlers in the area. He eventually ran one of the larger plantations, worked by several enslaved Blacks. Some of his slaves recalled how they "always had plenty of clothes and lots to eat" and they "all lived in good log cabins we built."

But Legus Perryman had never been a slave. Lewis Perryman, a non-Black Creek man, married Ellen Winslett, a Black Creek woman, who too had never been enslaved. She gave birth to Legus in Sodom (now known as Tullahassee), Oklahoma, a former all-Black town. Today Lewis Perryman is considered to be one of the fathers of the city of Tulsa. Legus's brother would go on to found Tulsa's first post office and serve as its postmaster. Legus became a lawyer and served as a prosecutor and judge. He then was elected to a seat in the Creek Nation House of Warriors.

Sharon Lenzy-Scott's direct ancestors founded Tulsa; they did so as "Tulsey Town." According to historians of the Brookside neighborhood, one of Tulsa's wealthiest neighborhoods today, "the mixed blood Creek Nation Perryman family was one of the first families to settle in this area and operated the first post office in 1882 at the home of George Perryman near what is now 41st & Trenton."

Perryman himself served in the Union Army as part of the 1st Regiment Indian Home Guards. While his older kin, Cow Tom, led the Creek Nation, Legus and his brothers Josiah and George took up arms and fought for the Union during the Civil War.

The Civil War was a pivotal time in marking and delineating color lines in the Creek Nation. It was because the mixed-blood Creeks fought in the Confederate Army that the full-bloods remained loyal to the Union. At least this was the contention made by Legus

Perryman, who was chief of the Creek Nation from 1887 to 1895 and lived for many years near what is now Tulsa. It was Legus with whom Senator Henry L. Dawes of Massachusetts dealt when negotiating a treaty with the Creeks when the Dawes Commission was first established in Indian Territory in 1893.

Although a full-blood Creek, Chief Perryman spoke English fluently and was as familiar with the history of white men in Indian Territory as he was with that of the Indians. He was one of the original claimants for a share in the loyal Creek payment, a fund distributed by the federal government among Indians who had remained loyal to the Union during the Civil War.

So Legus not only negotiated with Senator Dawes and what became known as the Dawes Commission but also was loyal to the Union cause, and for that he received significant financial support from the federal government, eventually leasing his land in Tulsa that would pasture approximately twenty-two thousand head of cattle for Texas ranchers.

Before he died, ex-chief Perryman explained the attitude of the Creek Indians during the Civil War. He said the first Creeks who emigrated to Indian Territory, per the stipulations of its treaty with the United States, were part of what was known as the McIntosh party, or mixed element. Full-blood Creeks were slower to leave their homes in the Southeast and didn't readily accept new conditions offered by the government, so they did not come to Indian Territory until 1832. This caused a breach between the two elements within the Nations, prompting the mixed-bloods to align against the full-bloods in nearly every political struggle.

At the start of the Civil War the McIntosh faction allied with the Confederacy. The full-bloods, being opposed to anything that the mixed-blood element supported, joined the Union Army. This explained, according to Perryman, why nearly all the Creeks who fought for the Union were full-bloods. Many mixed-bloods held slaves before the war, while few full-bloods did. This made it natural for the McIntosh to support the Confederate cause.

In other words, full-bloods included people like Legus Perryman who were both Creek and Black. Blackness, in Legus's eyes, didn't contaminate his Blackness or his Creekness. Mixed blood meant that you were mixed with white people and likely to be aligned with those who used slave labor and supported the Confederate cause.

In Perryman's opinion, few Creek Indians joined the armies of the North and South for purely patriotic reasons. "I fought in both armies," said Perryman. "When the war broke out I joined the Confederate Army. At the expiration of my term I went home and thought no more of going into the army until I visited a Union camp near Flat Rock. The boys wore such nice uniforms and were so anxious to have me join as a scout in the Southern army, and my experience there came in handy. We were stationed at Ft. Gibson and made raids from there on small bands of Confederates but had no big battles. It was very dangerous warfare, for if the enemy caught you it meant death."

According to Perryman, the U.S. government sent proclamations to the chiefs of the Five Civilized Tribes at the outset of the Civil War asking them to take no part on either side of the struggle. The Indians were regarded as neutral, and the federal government did not want them to suffer loss of property as a result of the war.

"But we just couldn't keep out of the war," Perryman said later. "We had heard the old Indians tell stories of valor and of brave deeds in wars with white men and with other tribes of Indians. A young man until he had undergone the dangers of war was not considered a complete citizen. The spirit of war had been so instilled into some of us that we were burning with a desire to ride a charger and face the bullets of the enemy. This caused most of the younger Creeks to take a hand in the war on one side or the other."

When the war ended, the Perryman boys went back to Tulsa with their allotments and their earned Union-loyalty dollars—Josiah and George to the Perryman business interests in and around Tulsa, while Legus went into law and politics. By 1868, he was elected to serve for six years as a district judge in the Coweta District. Before he was forty years old, he left the bench and was elected to a seat in the House of Warriors representing Big Spring Town when his brother Sanford died. During his time, he also sat on the Creek National Council. And he was reelected three times after first getting his brother's seat.

By 1887, Perryman was a household name in the Creek Nation and won easily the role of principal chief. As principal chief, Perryman dealt with the U.S. government—including Senator Dawes and his commission members. He negotiated with white settlers and had a front-row seat to the radical transformation of Indian Territory, which was rapidly moving toward becoming a state. With large landholdings overseen by his family, his extensive business interests, and his family's political involvement in the Creek Nation, Legus was clearly part of a dynastic power family. So how did Legus go from being part of what could be considered a Creek political dynasty to being, as the *New-York Tribune* quoted a political opponent in 1903, "a sly old coon"? And the opponent admitted, "I was mighty sorry old Legus got nominated, 'cause he ain't full blood Injin."

How did a Creek chief whose family for generations had been leaders in Indigenous Oklahoma politics become an "old coon"?

Legus Perryman was asked by the House Subcommittee for Indian Affairs in 1906 to speak on the restrictions the federal government had placed on full-blood Creeks to sell land they owned. Perryman was a full-blood according to the Dawes Rolls. Also known as the "Final Rolls," these are the lists of individuals who were accepted as eligible for tribal membership in the Five Civilized Tribes: Cherokees, Chickasaws, Choctaws, Creeks, and Seminoles. However, the lists do not include those whose applications were stricken, rejected, or judged as doubtful. Perryman was restricted for twenty-five years by federal law from selling the land he owned.

Being Black as well as being Creek was a recurring problem for those who were both. In the United States, one drop of Black blood made Perryman less Creek, less entitled to the rights and privileges of citizenship. Despite the other aspects of Legus's identity—Black Creek, lawyer, judge, landowner, leader—he was reduced to being labeled an "old coon." And being labeled that in a time when Black Codes, Jim Crow laws, and other codifications of white supremacy permeated every corner of life, Legus couldn't be anything else.

White supremacists worked to confirm this definition. Toward the end of his time as chief, Legus became known in news outlets as sly, scheming, and corrupt. In *The Guthrie Daily Leader* of May 24, 1904, the insinuation that Perryman was unscrupulous was made clear: "The loyal Creeks will soon receive the cash on their old war claims. The entire amount of the original claim was $1,200,000, but after long years of waiting and many conferences between the Indians and congressional committees it was finally scaled to half that amount. The Indian most instrumental in securing the award was Hon. D.M. Hodge, of Tulsa. For his services he was allowed to retain 5 per cent of the amount collected. This circumstance alone shows that the Indian but had little hopes of ever getting anything out of the government. The claim was pending more than thirty years. . . . Ex-Governor L.C. Perryman will get a nice little slice."

This is what happens when you're a Black leader of an institution not considered suitable for Black people, even if Black people helped build it. Cow Tom and Harry Island had negotiated the very treaties that kept alive the hopes of Black life in the Creek Nation. Cow Tom even led the Creek Nation when many in the Nation were considered refugees within the United States. But today, more than 150 years later, Black Creeks are still trying to convince the Nation that they belong. Reporters from the *Fort Worth Daily Gazette* put it this way in 1887:

> These Indians can not afford to quarrel and fight among themselves. If they expect to retain their tribal nationalities and existence, they must cultivate harmony among themselves. They must stand shoulder to shoulder. Avaricious whites stand ready to take advantage of all dissensions, to promote discord, division, and the opening up of the country. In union and harmony only is there prosperity and political salvation.

But before writers like Alex Posey hurled racist insults at Legus Perryman throughout his tenure as principal chief, plans were being hatched in the halls of white privilege. Senator Dawes, on the second day of the 1886 Lake Mohonk Conference—an annual meeting of wealthy white elites to discuss Indian affairs and make recommendations to the government—said: "When that time comes there can be no reservation to abolish or to perpetuate; no Indian agent to appoint or dismiss; no treaty to keep or abrogate. The work is accomplished when the Indian has become one of us, absorbed into this body politic, a self-supporting citizen, and nothing is left of these questions that are troubling us."

How did we get here? Who did this? Whose acts of seemingly benevolent white supremacy minimized Legus Perryman?

The classifications of race that limited him and thousands of other Black Creeks to imprecise, ahistorical identities that plagued Legus's direct descendant Sharon and her mother, Adlene, in 1979 are faulty at best.

And that's what Dawes did. As a white man elected to the U.S. Senate who was given the responsibility of determining what the relationship between the federal government and Native Nations should be going forward, he gave many nonwhites identities that we never asked for but that white supremacy required. These Creek rolls are the work of Dawes, and his actions haunt Cow Tom's descendants today.

CHAPTER 8

THE INVASION OF DAWES, CURTIS, AND BIXBY TOO

> The worst feature of the Indian service is that
> the Indian sometimes does not know what is best
> for him; and when he does know, ten chances
> to one he listens to the wrong man.
>
> HENRY DAWES

It is difficult to know true freedom when its boundaries are established by an oppressor. But that is the story of the Creek, and the stories of the Black and the Brown. The reason the Creek identity will always encompass the narrative of Indigenous and Black survival is that they share an oppressor.

When I delve into the history of the Five Tribes, Henry Dawes's name comes up over and over. But behind Dawes was a man named

Tams Bixby, who set in place much of the racism and white supremacy that Black Creeks face today. And Bixby, like many other destructive people with a benevolent veneer, has a town named after him too.

WE MIGHT HAVE THOUGHT that the work of "civilizing" had concluded with Benjamin Hawkins. But Henry Dawes saw it as his duty to instruct the Native Americans that the work of "civilizing" themselves was far from finished. Henry Dawes was the epitome of a northeastern elite. Born in western Massachusetts in 1816, he studied law at Yale and at thirty-two was elected to the Massachusetts House of Representatives. Two years later, he was elected to the state senate. And three years after that, he sat on the Massachusetts Constitutional Convention. He became a U.S. senator in 1874 at age fifty-eight.

Dawes was called by many white people of his time the "friend of the Indian." But who was this man who forever changed the landscape of Indigenous life in America and subsequently Black life forever?

While his career was distinguished on paper, it and he cannot be understood without understanding that he was more than anything a child of the age of scientific racism.

Consider where America was at the time that Dawes came to national power. Not more than a generation had passed since the Civil War. Industry had picked up. Railroads had begun to crisscross the land. Bit by bit, parts of the country that knew nothing of industry or capitalism were thrust into both. Immigrants by the millions poured into the country. People who once knew only how to till, sow, and reap found themselves moving away from the land to work in cities and factories. America was moving and it was moving fast.

In the eyes of many, humanity was progressing. Humanity was on part of its inevitable evolutionary pathway to improve: to get richer, move faster, live more comfortably. The assumption was that who we are now would be infinitely better than who we've been— and that who we can become would be orders of magnitude better than who and where we are now. Anthropologists, scientists, politicians, public intellectuals, and more got behind this concept. That America—tattered though it may have been a handful of decades ago—was on the proverbial come-up.

But there was a problem with this idea. These advances were not experienced by everyone. In fact, a great many people in the United States—some of whose ancestors predated the presence of white people in America—were not progressing at the rate that people expected. For these "civilized" white people who thought America was destined for progress, there were stages to culture—culture and cultural progress came in waves. According to social historian Frederick Hoxie, some of the leaders of the time thought that "racial differences raised the barriers between stages of culture." Two of them, William John McGee and William Henry Holmes, studied ways that culture could be advanced. As Holmes put it, "the final battle of the races for the possession of the world [was at that time] already on." Holmes accepted wholeheartedly that America would never be able to balance its teeming social progress with divergent paths of civilization and development between races, leading him to predict that there would inevitably be a "fading out to total oblivion" for people like the Indians, whom he called "savage" and "barbaric."

Who was Holmes? Who was William John McGee? And why does either of them matter?

Social progress was part of the appetite of Henry Dawes and the rest of the Dawes Commission, as was the belief that race and ethnicity were stumbling blocks to America's progress. People like Dawes believed that they could usher wayward Blacks and Natives toward civilization—white civilization.

WILLIAM JOHN MCGEE was a self-taught geologist, an inventor, and the author of numerous books. He was part of the U.S. Geological Survey in an era when the United States was expanding. He studied earthquakes and presented his findings at expositions. He led the American Association for the Advancement of Science (AAAS), the American Anthropological Association, and the National Geographic Society, and he cofounded the Geological Society of America. His influence was and still is undeniable.

McGee told the AAAS in 1897 about progress and the AAAS members' roles in it as bringing "order out of that vast chaos of action and thought which [had] so long resisted analysis and synthesis."

So how could he explain why whites in America had persistently been much more successful than their nonwhite counterparts? Easily. There were different groups of humanity. In McGee's explanation, "The progenitors of the white man must have been well past the critical point before the progenitors of the red and the black arose from the plane of bestiality to that of humanity."

In other words, the reason, in the minds of people like McGee, that white people have progressed so much faster than Black or Indigenous people is that they evolved faster than either group. And conversely, Black people, for McGee, have not evolved as quickly because they were predisposed to slower progress—if they experienced progress at all.

Black people are the cause of their own strife? Sound familiar? McGee added that "progress was neither uniform—whites evolved before blacks—nor steady. The races of the world might be blending into a single entity, but this was occurring through the more rapid extinction of lower races."

McGee went on to call America and its imperialistic appetite the "lamp of civilization" that shone bright on the "dark-skinned peoples" and believed that not all of us "barbarians" could be saved.

The story of progress for Black, Indigenous, and those who were both would come at the *allowance of white men*—if we were lucky enough to be "saved." And saving was truly a matter of luck meeting opportunity. As McGee said in a speech to the Anthropological Society of Washington, "the savage . . . stands strikingly close to sub-human species in every aspect of mentality. The range from the instinct and budding reason of higher animals to the thinking of lowest man seems far less than separating the zoomimic [animal-like] savage from the engine using inventor." The disposition of McGee mattered and still matters, because it foundationally influenced how leading thinkers and policy makers framed policies that influenced who they perceived as "savages."

Policy makers like McGee, Dawes, and Bixby were hungry for a scientific validation of their savior complex. So they made Blacks, Indians, and Black Indians in need of salvation. As Dawes wrote, "It is a pretty hard thing to deal with the character of men who refuse to see what is the best thing for them . . . the worst feature of the Indian service is that the Indian sometimes does not know what is best for him; and when he does know, ten chances to one he listens to the wrong man." This was scientific racism, and it fueled Dawes and others on the commission.

McGee was supposed to lead the Bureau of American Ethnology, but instead William Henry Holmes was given the position. Holmes was a self-trained museum curator who went on to write about civilizing humanity: "We are now able to foretell the fading out to total oblivion in the very near future. All that will remain to the world of the fated race will be a few decaying monuments, the minor relics preserved in museums, and something of what has been written." He believed that the fate of Indian culture would be left behind. In his writing, when he did refer to Blacks and Indians or Black Indians, he called them "inferior" and "uncivilized."

McGee and Holmes were not alone. A host of others also worked to perpetuate these ideas. In *American Anthropologist*, George Painter wrote that "it is proverbially true that primitive peoples cannot stand an enforced civilization. No better example of this can be cited than that of the American Indians, who, even on their own soil, have resisted civil conditions unto death. Indeed, they seem almost incapable of existence apart from their primitive, normal barbarism. Even where they have, in small numbers, settled to the arts of civilization, this is usually of such crude order and so much of their native habits and traditions are carried into it that they can be at best said to be only partially civilized."

Painter believed that the efforts of people like Benjamin Hawkins had failed not because Hawkins and his friends were wrong for trying to eradicate the remnants of American Indian culture and society but because they were doomed from the beginning: these people could not escape what Hawkins deemed their "normal barbarism."

In other words, the effort to make the Native American "white" had failed. For Painter, these efforts had failed so significantly that these tribes "seem surely destined to ultimate extinction."

But Painter wasn't done with his white-lensed survey of humanity, specifically the portions of humanity that sit on the margins. In 1919, Painter wrote in *American Anthropologist* that "the negro, as a slave, had a peculiar advantage over the Indian, in that he fell at once under the tutelage and compelling hand of the master race, already highly schooled in civilization. Thus, he was at once forced into a certain conformity with the fundamentals of a higher life and its allied habits were speedily acquired. Under slavery also he was more comfortably clothed and systematically fed than he had ever been in his native country."

Black people also benefited from slavery, Painter argued, because they got to learn how to be civilized up close by watching their white owners.

These were the leading American thinkers of the day, white men who shaped America's national culture about the "primitive." Their views fueled the nation's systemic white supremacy. This is how Black people and Indigenous people, and Black Indigenous people, became worthy of saving in white eyes.

These ideas didn't save anyone; they actually hurt these people with a benevolent brand of white supremacy armed with charity—a dangerous and alluring oppression. But to do this well, they had to craft a race where one didn't exist. They had to reduce Indian Nations to a race to subjugate them, and the way for America to do this to its own Indigenous peoples was through blood.

. . .

BARBARA FIELDS, a historian, and Karen Fields, a sociologist, published a book in 2012 that helped us understand why thinkers like George Painter became convinced of the seemingly embedded differences between white people and nearly everyone else. Racecraft, to Barbara and Karen Fields, is the idea that differences between races are rooted in "the eugenicist, biological racist notion that something—whether it is blood or genes—has created a set of scientifically distinct groupings of people." As Karen Fields said in an interview: "Racecraft encompasses the fact that the race that is pictured by the subjects as real in fact is not; it's made to be real and envisioned collectively as something real. People begin to think, 'I have a racial identity, I have a race. As a black person or white person, I have certain characteristics: I'm smart; I deserve to be at the bottom, and so on.' These things are programmed into people through the activity of doing that first thing, the act that is ostensibly based on heritage. That puts somebody in his or her place."

The faux science that undergirded racism was the notion that Black people, Native Americans, and Blacks who were also Native Americans were disposed to be evolutionarily behind. Karen Fields illuminates why an idea so distant from reality or any substantiated fact could ever take root: "Racecraft shares characteristics with witchcraft, two in particular. First, there's no rational causality." Nothing fundamentally associated with being Black or Native American or both could causally explain what people like McGee and others saw as less evolved. Fields refers to witchcraft because the women of the Salem Witch Trials had nothing about them that could causally explain why the men around them would describe them as witches. But she continues, "Second, there's (witting or unwitting) reliance on circular argument. For example, blood serves as a metaphor of race but is often taken as a feature of race, even by scientifically trained people. . . . If everyone takes race for granted, there's no reason that scientists would wean themselves from doing the same. Race is the category they start and end with." So in the case of Black people or Indigenous people, their Blackness and their Indigeneity became enough of an explainer of anything that Black people or Indigenous people would do or have done to them. This is how people have invented and built racism. It is how racism becomes durable.

For the leaders in the late 1800s and early 1900s who tried to reconstitute who should be "American," race was the category they started and ended with. Some of Dawes's contemporaries took the approach that Black and Native lives weren't worth much. Dawes and others viewed their roles as reformers, believing that these scientifically flawed people could be systematically improved. And it didn't just apply to Native Americans—it also applied to Black people. Dawes once said that the Republican Party needed to "deliver an embattled minority from tyrannical rule." In other words, Black people needed to be saved from slavery. But once they had been saved from tyranny, Dawes focused on another group: America's Indigenous people, specifically the Five Tribes. According to Kent Carter, an expert on Dawes's life and work, "Dawes was no doubt sincere in his desire to help the Indians," but it's often the unrequested help that does the most damage.

Dawes in 1887 tried to push through the General Allotment Act, which would give Native Americans, as Angie Debo put it, "the perilous gift of [American] citizenship." What became known as the Dawes Act sought to divide Indigenous, communally held lands. This forced these Nations, according to historian Kent Blansett, to "assume a capitalist and proprietary relationship with property." Dawes believed that this legislation "provided economic stability to reservation communities and promoted the process of assimilation." And what did that lead to? "The act liquidated tribal lands, while individual ownership further aided in the checker-boarding effect of many reservations." In other words, Indigenous-held land in Indian Territory (which is now Oklahoma) got smaller by about a hundred million acres, and the lands the Nations formerly held the federal government sold off to white settlers bent on making a profit mainly through ranching, farming, and leasing.

Such "helping" had even more dire consequences.

The Dawes Act sought to erode the sovereign power of tribal governments. Blansett shows that the allotments that were formerly communal turned private and led to "bank foreclosures, confisca- tion by the Internal Revenue Service, and fraudulent lease arrange- ments." Ownership of these lands would be subject to courts, where "they often were subdivided into tiny parcels, insufficient to support the [Indian, Black, and Black Indian] owners."

Perhaps the most insidious part of the Dawes Act is that it em- powered the federal government to determine who would get what. As a result, the government got to craft a race. As Sandy Grande, a political scientist and expert in Native American and Indigenous studies, put it, "the task of defining 'Indian-ness' was assigned to the Dawes commission, a delegation of white men who embraced the prevailing racial purity model, to express 'Indian-ness' in terms of blood quantum." "Blood quantum" is a highly dubious measurement of the amount of "Indian blood" one has; in other words, quantum is a fraction of blood that is derived from original enrollees of a tribe who were on tribal census rolls. The assumption was that those who were original enrollees were typically full-blood quantum. But even today, the U.S. Department of the Interior issues an ID card called the Certificate of Degree of Indian Blood (CDIB). And the blood quantum got its governmental start with Dawes, no matter how unscientific and unrelated to DNA it might be. So the way that blood quantum is calculated is by using tribal documents, and usually it's a tribal official or a government official who calculates it. As Grande goes on to say, "Since there was no 'scientific' means of determining precise bloodlines, commission members often ascribed blood status based on their own racist notions of what it meant to be Indian—designating full-blood status to 'poorly assimilated' Indians and mixed-blood status to those who most resembled whites."

These designations are still in place today, barring the descendants of Cow Tom from what is owed them: their identity.

Before the Dawes Act, the Creek Nation was a confederacy of different tribes and peoples, embracing and amalgamating in their own way, mixing cultures and identities, living with the peace and controversy that any sovereign Nation with different types of people does. But as Barbara Fields and Karen Fields suggest, that's what racecraft does: it conjures the characteristics that are not actually tied to race but are linked to it to define race categories and their subsequent treatment. That was what Dawes's efforts gave us. Dawes crafted a race, one whose bounds were limited to what he and a group of white men thought this new Indian race would be and how this newly crafted race could serve their interests. It was no longer tradition, heritage, honor, self-determination, and pride that wove these people groups together.

This is why it is puzzling for you to hear today of people who were both Black and Indian. It seems contradictory because we have been taught that even a drop of Blackness can dilute whatever other elements of identity there are in people. Why? Back in the early 1900s when the Dawes Commission was enrolling people, those with mixed Freedmen and Indian parents were automatically enrolled as Freedmen, just as Cow Tom's descendants like Jake Simmons Sr. were. And that drop of Freedman identity crowded out their traces of Indian "blood." It stripped them of the identity of these Black people whose identities were forged in Creek traditions. Being both fully Creek and fully Black seems nearly impossible, and Dawes's work made it even more difficult for Cow Tom's descendants to be recognized as that.

So how did we get here? And who helped Dawes "help" so many people?

WHEN THE MEMBERS of the Five Tribes made the long march across the Trail of Tears, they did it with the understanding that this would be the last time their land would be minimized and curtailed. But when racism, anti-Indigenous politics, and the desire to maximize the white man's financial gains come together, past commitments loosen.

At the end of the Civil War, as the federal government tried to consolidate its power in the South, while Blacks were freed from slavery, they were soon subjected to what were known as Black

Codes. These restrictive state laws were enacted to restrain Black people's freedom and nearly guaranteed to land-owning whites the use of Black people as cheap (free) labor. While the number of Black elected officials in the South increased, there were limits placed on Black voting: even Lincoln wanted to place limits on Black suffrage. In states like South Carolina, Blacks were hit hard with discriminatory tax penalties that pummeled their economic well-being. These codes sowed the seeds for what would later become the laws and practices known as Jim Crow.

This was happening while the federal government was trying to keep pace with the rapid development of the American economy, which was rebounding after the war. As burgeoning railroads brought people west, undiscovered lands (by white men) were prospected and explored, and every measure of past treaties was scrutinized.

The railroad companies began to creep toward Indian Territory. And with them came immigrants from the North and the East. Settling around railroad tracks, these people—soon to be encroachers—saw the vast undeveloped lands and the opportunities that previous generations had seen in the southeastern United States. But they also saw Blacks who lived among Indians, and some Indians who didn't want anything to do with some other Indians.

That is where Dawes reappeared. He came to count, divide, and minimize nonwhite people in Indian Territory.

Friend to Native Americans though he claimed to be, his intentions were clear—and destructive. Perhaps Dawes, who by November 1, 1893, had retired from the Senate, and his commission comrades Meredith Kidd (a Democrat and former military leader) and Archibald McKennon (a former Confederate commanding officer) had every intention of allowing the Five Tribes to "civilize" at their own pace. But Interior Secretary Hoke Smith, to whom the commission reported, had more strident ideas, which he expressed in a twenty-five-page letter called "General Letter of Instructions." Secretary Smith wrote to Dawes, "Success in your negotiations will mean the total abolition of the tribal autonomy of the Five Civilized Tribes and the wiping out of the quasi-independent governments within our territorial limits. It means, also, ultimately, the organization of another territory in the United States and the admission of another state or states in the Union."

Where did Hoke Smith get this determination?

Congress in 1870 started to allow railroads to crisscross the continent. Many of those tracks were put down in Oklahoma and with them came, as one Cherokee put it, "the intrusion of whites [which] became not only easy but almost spectacular." Kent Carter, author of *The Dawes Commission and the Allotment of the Five Civilized Tribes, 1893–1914*, wrote that "the Five Civilized Tribes were inundated by white farmers, merchants, miners, railroad construction crews, speculators, whiskey peddlers, and a wide assortment of criminals attracted by advertisements promising great opportunities." The Creeks called these people "intruders." Today, if they were Brown, some would disparagingly call them "illegal immigrants." Instead, we called them "pioneers." Some called them what my alma mater calls them: "Sooners." "Numerous towns that had sprung up along the railroad lines presented a special problem because almost all of their residents were non-citizen whites who insisted that they be given the right to buy the lots on which they had built homes," according to Carter. And how could white settlers buy such lots, unless the United States removed the Indian hold on those lands?

Senators came to visit Indian Territory and concluded that the problems were not caused by white settlers—the very "illegal immigrants" who invited themselves into this Indian Territory. It was somehow the fault of the Five Nations that they couldn't keep their houses in order. These senators argued in court that the current Native land treaties were unfair to white people and said that the three hundred thousand uninvited whites living in Indian Territory were sending their children to schools that were deplorable. In their view, it was the responsibility of these Native Americans to run schools that were of high quality for the white interlopers.

These senators concluded that the Native American "system of government cannot continue. It is not only non-American, but it is radically wrong, and change is imperatively demanded in the interest of the Indian and whites alike, and such change cannot be much longer delayed. The situation grows worse and will continue to grow worse." Hoke Smith's instructions were clear: the U.S. government was reducing the Indian Territory even further. And Dawes came to reduce it further still for the Native Americans.

Angie Debo said that "the United States had finally determined to break down the autonomy of the Five Tribes and erect a white man's state upon the ruins of the Indian governments." This was the moment that white men in America had been waiting for.

The president at the time, Grover Cleveland, approved, but he wanted at least a modicum of consent from the Nations and believed that Dawes was the best man to elicit that consent—emphasizing that they "would not listen to anybody" but him.

Dawes alerted the Nations that he was coming. And the Nations and their leaders, one of them Black—Legus Perryman—were vehemently opposed. All the while Congress started to assume that tribal governments had to be reduced to nothing because they had, as Colorado senator Henry Teller noted, "wholly perverted their high trusts. They have demonstrated their incapacity to so govern themselves, and no higher duty can rest upon the Government that granted this authority than to revoke it when it has lamentably failed." For Teller and others, these tribal governments were antiquated at best, and at worst they were stopping the overall progress of the United States.

By 1894, Dawes and the commissioners tried to set up meetings with the Five Nations. Tribal chiefs, Legus included, refused for months to respond to letters. Eventually they did for the same reason that negotiations happened in the past: either you negotiated the means of your own destruction to slow its pace or you refused and were overwhelmed by it.

After meeting with tribal leaders, Dawes recommended in 1897 making "order out of that vast chaos of action and thought which [had] so long resisted analysis and synthesis." And Dawes knew just how that order would come: count and divide.

How would this happen? Allotment.

WHEN THE ALLOTMENT BILL was passed by Congress, it empowered Dawes and his commission to decide who would be Indian, to what degree people would be Indian, and who was not.

Imagine white men coming to you and dictating what your customs and traditions should be on the land you own. They give you slavery, a practice you don't want, especially not in the form that they practice. After you realize that these white men are increasing in number, you come to understand that resisting outright is futile. So you negotiate, only to see that you can only slow the inevitable tide of "civilization" that will wash over you. These whites tell you to leave your homes and march hundreds of miles on a deadly odyssey that your descendants will one day barely learn about in school. You go with the explicit understanding from the president that you and your Nation will never have to move again, that you will never be displaced again. But a civil war happens around you and the world comes apart. Some of you are conscripted to fight, some of you on both sides, forcing you to learn the delicate dance of diplomacy. The war ends and the world is in chaos. Again white men illegally enter your lands and demand that you educate them and make your land and your governance familiar to them no matter how it inconveniences you.

Now comes the final invasion.

As Dawes aged and his health faded, the question arose: Who could replace this man who oversaw the radical contraction of Indian Territory? It must be someone who could further "civilize" the Native American in the twentieth century. His name was the name of a city less than a mile from where I grew up.

"Henry Dawes may have given the commission its name, but Tams Bixby defined its character and would serve as its leader during the critical period of enrollment and allotment," Kent Carter wrote, "and he would make the daily decisions that affected the life and future of all of the people in Indian Territory." And not long before that, when people wrote to the commission, they'd often address it to the "Dawes-Bixby Commission." Tams Bixby became so popular that "land promoters named a townsite after him, and some parents even named their children Tams, probably in hopes of ensuring a favorable decision on their enrollment applications."

By the end of the 1890s, as Dawes was gliding into old age, Bixby and others on the commission were busy implementing the Dawes Rolls, an even more bastardized census to count who in the eyes of the U.S. government was a citizen of the Five Nations, who wasn't, and how much land people would get. Many Creeks did not want to participate in the census, so the commission team relied on the word of "town kings"—akin to city managers, small-town mayors, or city councillors—and their friends and relatives. Imagine entrusting a mayor or city manager to attest to your identity. But when a hunger for making money from the eventual sale of land that people weren't supposed to own in the first place is the primary lure, people will use any means necessary to run over the marginalized for their own benefit.

It wasn't long before the commission's leader began to receive letters from people from all over the United States "asking how they could get on the rolls so they could get Indian land." Armed with the threat that they could do this with or without Indigenous help, the Dawes Act was amended by the Curtis Act.

Passed in 1898 and signed into law by President William McKinley, the Curtis Act broke up the sovereign governments and lands of the Cherokee, Chickasaw, Choctaw, Creek, and Seminole. Initially the Five Nations were exempt from the 1887 Dawes Act because they had treaties with the United States that predated that act.

But throughout America's history, treaties with marginalized people have invariably been broken by white men. And break those treaties the government did.

Creek chief Isparhecher and the rest of the Creek National Council received notification that the United States hoped to enroll members of their Nation—to place them on a roll created by the U.S. government that the Nation would then use. Isparhecher rebuffed it, saying that his Nation was "astonished" by the suggestion and that Congress's granting the commission the authority to create rolls of his Nation's citizens was tantamount to a "grave violation of numerous treaty pledges made each of the Five Nations in oft-time repeated treaties."

Each of the Five Nations balked at the audacity of the United States to oversee the tribes' determining of who would be Indian and who would not. And you cannot blame them. It's like the United States invading another country and then telling that country who could be a citizen and who could not.

As Kent Carter remarked, "It is clear that some Creeks thought their [tribal] government could still negotiate with the United States as an equal, but they would soon learn that the federal government was not prepared to take 'no' for an answer." Some of the Creeks employed a strategy of ignoring the commission, much to their detriment as the tribal rolls kept growing without their consent or consultation.

So then came the Curtis Act, which wrested control of the enrollment process away from the Nations and placed it firmly in the hands of the U.S. government. The act gave the control of determining Nations citizenship to the Dawes Commission. As a result, the

Dawes Commission could now, without tribal consent and approval, dictate who was going to be Creek, sometimes resorting to eyeballing the complexions of applicants as a means of determining citizenship.

With the loss of control of the Nations' citizenship rights also came the eradication of the Nations' courts, conventions of tribal governance, and communal land claims that once existed in Indian Territory. This change helped to accelerate Indian Territory's becoming Oklahoma and the flood of white men profiting off land once held by Creek families.

The Dawes Commission created a Freedman Roll, which included all of the people who looked to the Dawes Commission's surveyors to be a drop too Black to be considered Creek. Before the Freedman Roll, all Creek members, Freedmen or not, were entitled to the same rights. Yet the Dawes Freedmen Roll made people like Damario Solomon-Simmons and his family too Black to be Creek.

And so began another long struggle.

When racecraft takes hold, it gives permission for people to turn on each other. Pleasant Porter replaced Legus Perryman as chief and began to hurl similar vitriol against his Black Creek brothers that white men directed toward Black people. Chief Porter testified before the Senate in 1906 and said of the Freedmen that they had "come forth from the four quarters of the earth and employ a lawyer here to assist them, and they and the lawyer will get up the proof that slides them through, and on the rolls they go. It is as slick as grease."

Even the term "Freedman" was damaging. Legus Perryman was a Black man who'd never been enslaved and who had led the Creek Nation. But by making him and his family Freedmen, the Dawes Commission anchored the Perrymans' identity to one that may have ever been theirs. The same can be said of Damario's family, who to this day believes that Cow Tom was never a slave. But their identity claims, their history, and their ability to determine who they are continue to be shackled by the term "Freedman."

Labeling these people as Freedmen did what the scientific racists needed: it created a category of people who were saved from the scourge of slavery by the "courageous" help of elites who saved Black people from the hell those elites had helped to create. While there is much more to Dawes's effect on life in Indian Territory, this much is clear: his involvement led to a wound from which Creeks would never recover. His actions were a clear expression of racism and racecraft in America—and they found their way inside one of the few places that had been able to keep at bay the marginalization of Black people.

CHAPTER 9

HIS HOLY GROUND

Where there is sorrow, there is holy ground.

OSCAR WILDE

I've always been intimidated by the term "holy." Growing up in a strict Christian household, I heard quotes from the Bible frequently. Holiness became a seemingly endless list of dos and don'ts—a vision of perfection that would forever go unfulfilled.

By age thirteen, I had picked up a knack for ancient languages like Latin and biblical Greek. Somewhere in the study of these I realized that "holiness" in the Greek doesn't mean perfect, it means "set apart." None of the religious artifacts in the Christian tradition that were considered high holy were perfect. These artifacts were imperfect, often unimpressive objects that were holy because they were set apart. Two planks of wood crossing each other. Nails driven into the feet and hands of a man named Jesus. Or intensely salty water from a sea they called "Dead."

The land owned by Jake Simmons Sr. was not perfect, but it was set apart. As land it is typical for eastern Oklahoma, but it is different from land found elsewhere. It is unique, embedded with the history that sets it apart. Holy.

IN 1937, the Great Depression was gutting the prosperity of Americans. By mid-1938, 19 percent of Americans were out of work. Industrial production had declined by nearly 30 percent. And global gross domestic product (GDP) had contracted by 18.2 percent.

To give people employment, President Franklin Delano Roosevelt created the Works Progress Administration (WPA) as part of the New Deal. Roosevelt appointed Henry Alsberg, a writer and journalist, to run a small program within the WPA called the Federal Writers' Project. The program employed more than ten thousand out-of-work writers with the mandate of crafting a "self-portrait of America."

Taking that self-portrait meant capturing the experiences of all types of Americans. Perhaps the least known treasure of the Federal Writers' Project is the WPA Slave Narrative Collection. In seventeen states, writers were deployed to meet with former slaves to capture and record their experiences.

Phoebe Banks, a distant relative of Damario, was seventy-eight in 1937 when writers employed by the Oklahoma Writers' Project, a subset of the Federal Writers' Project, interviewed her about her experiences as a former Black slave. Banks, one of the Creek Freedpeople—a former slave in the Creek Nation—recalled:

> My mother belonged to Mose Perryman when I was born;
> he was one of the best-known Creeks in the whole nation,

and one of his younger brothers, Legus Perryman, was made the big chief of the Creeks a long time after the slaves was freed. Mother's name was Eldee; my father's name was William McIntosh, because he belonged to a Creek Indian family by that name. Everybody say the McIntoshes was leaders in the Creek doings away back there in Alabama long before they come out here.

That same year, L. W. Wilson, another writer of the Oklahoma Writers' Project, interviewed Jake Simmons Sr., Damario's great-great-grandfather, whose story was radically different from Phoebe's. Like Phoebe, Jake Sr. was Creek, but unlike Phoebe, Jake was born a free Black man. By definition, Jake Sr. wasn't a "Freedman," because he had never been enslaved. In fact, Wilson was specifically tasked with talking to Jake Simmons to include his story in the Indian-Pioneer Papers Collection along with those of other Native Americans.

How did the story of a Black man find its way into a collection about Native Americans?

Perhaps the easiest answer is that Jake Simmons's land was sacred.

Phoebe Banks perfectly embodied the complex lost narrative of Blackness and Indigenous identity. Legus Perryman, her uncle and the uncle-in-law of Jake Simmons Sr., was the principal chief—effectively the president—of the Creek Nation in 1887. He was a Black man who was never owned by the Creeks. Instead, he led them. The other side of Phoebe's family, the McIntoshes, were adopted Creek slaves—in other words, they were accepted as members of the Creek Nation after being slaves. Today, the descendants of Creek slaves and descendants of Black members of the Creek Nation who were never enslaved are lumped into the broad category of "Creek Freedmen" who are no longer considered members of the Creek Nation.

IN THE DECADES after the Civil War thousands of recently freed Black people found themselves trying to figure out how they were going to live in America. What became clear is that life for them would not be what their white counterparts experienced. Their enduring struggle would be to find places where they could fit in.

That would not be the case for the Simmons family.

As Jake Simmons Sr. recalled, "The beginning of the Civil War found the Creek Indians in a very comfortable condition." By that point, "many white and colored people had married into the tribe and became citizens of the tribe." But it was clear to Jake Sr. that "slavery led to the outbreak of the Civil War between the states of the North and the states of the South, but the Creeks preferred to not take sides with either, remembering well how they lived and strived in the years past to climb to the top to acquire what they possessed and the peace that reigned among them."

Soon there was increasing pressure from both the Confederacy and the Union for the Creek Nation and its male citizens to join the fight. Jake admitted that his father initially joined the Confederate Army, but he never really took up arms. Instead, under the leadership of Opothle Yahola, a former chief of the Creek Nation, they fled to Kansas, which led the Confederates to believe that this faction of Creeks had joined the Union. The Confederates considered it a betrayal and targeted the Creeks for attacks. Inevitably the Creeks joined the Union cause and gathered, as Simmons remembered, "all of their earthly possessions"; they did not have "weapons to defend themselves in anything like comparison with those of the soldiers." So the journey to Kansas came as "they suffered loss untold."

For Jake, "the Civil War was one in which the Creek Indians" and "the other tribes would have not participated for they were not concerned but were subjects of persuasion. It was disastrous to them from start to finish, for their property was destroyed and many of them lost their lives and in the end much of their land was taken from them. Their slaves were set free which was of little loss compared with the other losses."

Reconstruction was in full swing during Jake's adolescence. The Creek Nation, as he remembered it, was decimated. "The closing of the war found the Creek Nation in a more pitiable condition than the rest of the Nations of the Five Tribes, due, as I have said, to . . . most activities of the war being centered in the Creek Nation. Homes destroyed, horses, oxen, and cattle killed or driven off."

He remembered that when he was a child, the work that his wife's grandfather Cow Tom did with the numerous treaty discussions gave slaves the same rights as other Creeks. However, because the work of Cow Tom did not directly affect him and because he was never a slave, it wasn't an issue for him and many like him. From Jake's perspective, the main activities of the Creek Nation after the Civil War were that "all tribes finally agreed with the Government that unused lands that had been theirs would be made into reservations for Indians of Kansas, Nebraska, and other places and that the negro slaves should be citizens of the tribes, rights-of-way granted for railroads and tribal Governments set up under . . . United States supervision."

Again when "liberation" was given, it came with restrictions. This was land to be run by the Creeks as a result of Indian Removal. Instead, the tribal governments had to be set up and maintained under the supervision of the United States.

"When the lands were given to other Indians it naturally reduced the acreage, and the negro also acquired ownership in the land as much as the Creeks themselves had enjoyed part of the tribal funds," Jake said. He didn't consider himself like the other slaves. Jake was fully a member of the Creek Nation, adopted in because his father was Creek and had married a Creek woman.

Despite this history, the Dawes Commission oversimplified this man's complex history and his family's involvement to one word: Freedmen.

Cow Tom's work for the Creek Nation and the Simmons family history were forced to fit into the white government's narrow and invented definitions. This distinction of "Freedman" didn't mean as much then as it does now. But it started a process of separation within the Creek Nation that continues today. Cow Tom ran the Creek Nation in its worst times. He represented the Creek Nation before the U.S. government and rescued the fate of Black people in the Creek Nation, and subsequently other Nations adopted similar principles. But all that one of Cow Tom's descendants, Jake Simmons Sr., could be in a Creek Nation whose rules were changed by white government was a "Freedman."

The word isn't even accurate. Like other Creeks, he could recall when the Creeks reestablished themselves after the Civil War. Like Pleasant Porter, who recalled what life was like before the Creek Nation was further forced to "civilize," Simmons remembered simpler times that weren't under the forced and unwanted tutelage of white America. "With their ax they set about cutting down trees and building log cabins and clearing land for cultivation," Jake said. "Some of these cabins were built of logs stood on ends, others were laid horizontally. The roofs were thatched (built of limbs and grass), some of the roofs were made of clapboards split out with the ax. They had no nails and these shingles or clapboards were held on by laying logs at intervals to hold them."

Jake was as Creek as Creek gets.

In addition, Jake Simmons married Rose Jefferson, a grand-daughter of Cow Tom, in 1884. Rose, like Cow Tom, was dark complected, her hue a rich African black. She was less interested in appearing more "American" and wore "cornrows wrapped with a scarf." She grew up working on her grandfather's farm. Her mother, Melinda, Cow Tom's daughter, wed a Black Creek political leader and moved onto Cow Tom's estate and took over running it when Cow Tom died in 1874. Rose was known for her beauty, her education, and her skills at running the house and ranch. After meeting her, then-nineteen-year-old Jake was impressed by what he found: "a sharp-witted, forceful dark-skinned woman."

Jake visited her in Okmulgee, the Creek capital, every chance he had, and they married on July 24, 1884. According to one report, Jake said, "I thought I was a man. I got married while my boss man was away on Saturday night, July 24, 1884, to John Jefferson's daughter by the name of Rose Jefferson; her father at that time was a wealthy colored man in this part of the country, but I kept on working and I didn't see my wife for two months although I was only twelve miles from her."

Jake himself had a significant Creek lineage of his own. His mother was a Black Creek woman named Lucy Perryman—from the same Perryman family that founded Tulsa. She was born to Creek royalty, as her father was Mose Perryman. He called himself "colored" and married Katie Harrison. Besides Lucy, they had two other children, Jane and Louisa. As an example of the absurd notion of racial distinction within the Nation, the Dawes Commission's administrative minions designated Jane as a "full-blood" and her sister Louisa as "Freedman." That is what happens when white people in power dictate the confines of your identity: they put you in boxes you don't belong in and have no control over. This is what America does to us. And these boxes make us far less than our white counterparts.

Jake's father, Jim, we know far less about. He had lighter skin through his father, Jake's grandfather, whom Jake sometimes called a white man or a Creek ranchman. Jim Simmons, his father, was born in Missouri and was adopted into the Cherokee Nation before the Civil War. Jake himself was born in a Confederate refugee camp while his father enlisted to fight for the Confederates, forbade his wife's interaction with her Black relatives, and eventually abandoned her.

Jake's mother bounced from place to place and finally let his grandmother Katie raise him. Jake had little formal education, but he found both opportunity and destiny in becoming a rancher.

But building up this land took time. In his youth he worked odd jobs, selling nuts, fishing, and delivering syrup until he ate too much of his own supply and was fired after getting sick. He learned to be a rancher the way scientists study their experiments: he observed successful cattle ranchers and drew conclusions on best practices. As he said: "I have from the time I was a little boy been interested in the

cattle business and I have studied it from every angle from its beginning to its present day. I never did much farming in my life; that is,
extensively as I have always worked on the range and ranches and
am still today engaged in the raising of cattle on my miniature ranch
of eleven hundred acres, compared with the ranches in my early
manhood."

His knowledge increased when he started working on the ranch
of Bluford Miller, one of the most successful cattle ranchers of the
time. When Jake was a teenager, about four years before he met
Rose, he and Miller, a fellow orphan, became friends. Miller was a
successful white man in the Creek Nation, and he ran stock up and
down the critical cattle trail that that ran between Kansas and Texas.
It was there that Jake Sr. learned the intricacies of ranching, eventually managing the financial side of Miller's ranch.

At the time, beef consumption was on the rise. Between 1880 and
1900, the U.S. beef industry nearly doubled in size. With that in-
crease came the radical growth of Miller's ranch, which Jake Simmons and others called Hart Ranch. The grass within the boundaries
of the Creek Nation was prime grazing land and was exactly what
the cattle needed to fatten. And fatten they did. Simmons spent weeks
on large roundups, managing men, animals, and finances, learning
as he went.

Simmons hoped one day to own and manage as large a ranch as
Bluford's, but he knew that his lack of capital was an impediment
and that his family wanted him to marry a woman with position,
like Rose Jefferson, the granddaughter of Cow Tom. According
to one of Jake Simmons's grandchildren, Jake married Rose "because she was nearly all African and her family had no history of

slavery—he didn't want his children raised with those kinds of feelings, that they were less of human beings than anyone else . . . [and] she had a lot of money."

Simmons was proud of the way his wife looked, once exclaiming (according to family members), "I may have white skin but my wife, Rose, is as black as tar and I'm proud of it . . . stand up so everyone can see how beautiful your black skin is!"

Their married life seemed to run out of luck before it had even started. "I struck out for myself in 1886 and tried farming," Simmons said. "Everything looked bright at first but about the time my crops were laid by, a big hailstorm came along and tore up nearly everything that had been planted and left me almost flat."

With an $80 loan and Miller's support, Simmons got back on his feet. Soon he took up "a contract to furnish 18,000 rails, to be bought and delivered at [another guarantor's] expense." That led to a $100 payout. He took his hard-won knowledge as a farm and ranch hand and raised cattle for the Choctaw Nation and eventually on his own ranch. Rose's citizenship in the Creek Nation entitled her (and her enterprising husband) to land. Starting with the standard 160 acres allotted to Rose, Cow Tom enlarged it over time. And the pride Simmons took in his success beamed off the pages of *The Southern Workman* when the magazine published a profile of him in 1915. "Today I run my own ranch, have my own farm with about 1800 acres of land, and cultivate 700 acres. I have a large barn and 270 head of cattle."

And he wasn't done.

"My barn is 65 by 80 feet, and there are two or three other outbuildings 60 by 20 feet. I sell about $5,000 worth of cattle of my own and buy and sell many thousands dollars' worth more for others at a good profit—between seven and eight thousand dollars' worth." .

These numbers are more impressive when you understand that in 1900, the average worker made $449.80 per year and the average Black male laborer took home about $150. By 1920, the annual amounts earned by Black families in Harlem at the height of the Harlem Renaissance was approximately $1,300.

The year after Jake Simmons's appearance in *The Southern Workman*, America began to witness the Great Migration of what became nearly six million Black people leaving the South for opportunities in the West, up North, and in the big cities of the Midwest. They were, as Isabel Wilkerson put it, chasing the warmth of other suns.

But Jake Simmons chose to stay in Oklahoma because the warmth of his sun was generated by his lineage and that of his wife. He said that he had sold that year $5,000 of his own cattle on land that sprawled nearly eighteen hundred acres. The equivalent of $5,000 today would be approximately $127,000. He also indicated that his other activities netted him $7,000 to $8,000 in profit, which today would be more than $200,000. The 2018 median annual salary of a farmer was $66,360.

On his land, Jake said, "There [were] about nine families on my place; I keep about seven or eight working hands all the time; and am now working about twenty, being very busy with my hay work.

"When first starting out I lived in a chicken house twelve by fourteen feet. Now I own a ten-room residence, comfortably furnished and in a settlement where we have a good school, a good church, and plenty of amusement." Jake and Rose Simmons, with the school and their upgraded mills, had become the fulfillment of Cow Tom's dreams of a grist mill and a school for his posterity.

Too often we look at Black success stories and apply them to all Black people: if not every Black person is attaining what someone like Jake Simmons did, then something is wrong with all Black people. But Simmons's narrative was aided by an identity that didn't limit his Blackness but rather removed the shackles of limited opportunity and equipped his family with land and a firm stake of equality in the Creek Nation—chances that Black people rarely have had in America.

"There is no doubt about there being a fine chance for our Negro people to come out to Oklahoma and succeed in farming, stockraising, and other kinds of business," Jake said in *The Southern Workman*. "I think I have succeeded with little or no education. It stands to reason that some of the graduates of the industrial and agricultural schools ought to be able to do better than I have done."

PERHAPS THE CONVENERS of the Parsons Convention—a convening of Black men who had decided to make Oklahoma a Black state—read what Jake Simmons said or saw other statements when they decided that Oklahoma was the ideal place for Black people.

This hope for more land, with more land creating more opportunity, and more opportunity promising more freedom for both Black people and their posterity, wasn't unique to Black Creeks. It was top of mind for thousands of other Black people who pined for the day when they would get their piece of the pie—the so-called forty acres and a mule.

The year Jake Simmons was born, the Civil War was coming to

an end. General William Tecumseh Sherman issued Special Field Orders No. 15, which allowed for the repatriation of four hundred thousand acres in South Carolina, Georgia, and Florida owned by white landowners, to be divided into forty-acre packets. Each of those packets was to be distributed to eighteen thousand once-enslaved families and other Black people living in those states. It's where the phrase "forty acres and a mule" comes from. This notion reminds us that most of us haven't been compensated for the pain experienced. As W. E. B. Du Bois called it, we were "destined in most cases to bitter disappointment." In fact, when Andrew Johnson became president after Abraham Lincoln was assassinated, he reversed this order.

Compare that with what happened to Cherokee Freedmen, who were given land and guaranteed restitution. Dr. Melinda Miller, an economics professor at Virginia Tech, showed that Cherokee Black Freedmen fared far better than non-Cherokee Freedmen. Cherokee, like the Creek, fully integrated their Black citizens based on the treaty guidance negotiated by Cow Tom. Miller found that over the following decades Black Cherokee prospered, with "lower levels of racial inequality, higher incomes for blacks, higher literacy rates among blacks, and greater school attendance rates among blacks."

It was this prosperity, this opportunity, that attracted the attention of Black people who did not share the ancestry of the Five Nations that Jake and others do. In 1882, the Reverend W. B. Avery of Parsons, Kansas, stood before a group of about sixty Black men to give his recommendation. "We have come together to deliberate—or, in other words, for the purpose of devising ways and means by which our condition may be bettered."

This group had been convened to determine how to make good

on the promises made by the Freedmen's Bureau (an important agency, which, after the Civil War, directed "provisions, clothing, and fuel . . . for the immediate and temporary shelter and supply of destitute and suffering refugees and Freedmen and their wives and children") and Special Field Orders No. 15—to figure out what they would get in lieu of their forty acres and a mule. But the work and success of people like Jake Simmons led Avery to call "attention to the fertile lands in Oklahoma Territory." Why? Because of his hope, his prayer, "I propose to ask . . . for a loan and the privilege of entering the Oklahoma lands, and settling down for once." In Avery's opinion, Oklahoma was the place where he and his peers could "do our part in making America a second Eden."

The land of Oklahoma—Jake's land—wasn't perfect but it was holy. It was sacred because it stood apart.

If our imagination could be reframed with a more accurate brand of Black history and a sharper sense of Black identity, we would understand what all Black people in America are owed.

CHAPTER 10

LIVING THE DREAM, SURVIVING THE NIGHTMARES

The chances of success were slim indeed: creation of an
all-Black territory and eventually a state out of a hunk of
the United States already deeded to American Indians
and an object of lust for white settlers, cattlemen,
land speculators and railroaders.

RANDY KREHBIEL, REPORTER
FOR THE *TULSA WORLD*

E dward McCabe (who also went by Edwin McCabe) dreamed
a radical dream: that there could be an all-Black state in the
Union. Jake Simmons and his family lived that dream.

Fifteen years before Jake Simmons Sr. was born, Edward P. Mc-
Cabe was born in Troy, New York, almost fifteen hundred miles
away from the Simmons land in Haskell, Oklahoma. McCabe's family moved to Massachusetts, Rhode Island, and then to Maine. When

his father died in Maine, the family's moves ended, as did his school-ing. He took a job as a clerk on Wall Street and then headed west to Chicago to work with the godfather of Chicago's State Street and Lake Shore Drive, Potter Palmer. By age twenty-two, McCabe was appointed clerk in the then Cook County Office of the Federal Trea-sury. This rise is even more impressive when you learn that Edward McCabe was Black.

In the December 1978 issue of Kansas State University's *Minori-ties Resource and Research Center Newsletter*, Edward McCabe was featured: "Edward P. McCabe and the Movement for Black Self-Determination in West."

Edward's best friend was a free-born, never-enslaved Black man in Chicago named Abram Thomas Hall Jr. The son of an African Methodist Episcopal pastor, Abram was a darker-skinned man whose photographs radiate propriety even today. He was rarely caught not wearing his four- and five-button, three-piece suits and strong Windsor-knotted ties. His back always straight, he had a winsome smirk with eyes that kids today would call "smizing." As a free-born man with parents who were not slaves, Hall could choose who and what he wanted to be without the boundaries that come with being a slave.

Hall first enrolled in medical school to become a physician. After a year he left medical school and pursued sailing. A few years after that he settled on journalism. In Abram's estimation, Black people of his time had become entranced by "reports of boundless acreage, fertility of soil[,] equable climate and golden opportunity to acquire and own a home on lands west of the Missouri river, in the State of Kansas."

Abram persuaded Edward McCabe to leave Chicago for the

dream to live in the West. The two left Chicago in early spring 1878 and set their sights on Kansas, exhibiting, as Toni Morrison would later write, "how exquisitely human was the wish for permanent happiness and how thin human imagination became trying to achieve it."

Abram and Edward weren't alone in this search. Hundreds of other Black people moved to a small community in Graham County, Kansas, that was named after a tax collector from the Bible: Nicodemus. Between 1877 and 1879, six hundred Black people settled in Nicodemus, Kansas's only all-Black town that is still standing.

These six hundred people were part of a larger movement called the Exodusters. Their way was made possible by political action. In 1862, the United States passed the first of several Homestead Acts, which at first applied only to women and immigrants. But in 1866 another Homestead Act was passed that explicitly made it possible for Blacks to gain possession of nearly 160 million acres of land that had been opened up in the West by the U.S. government.

With the stroke of a pen, ownership of government land for formerly enslaved Black people became possible. Some who had escaped slavery and gone to Canada returned to take advantage of this new chance to be landowners. Benjamin "Pap" Singleton was one of them. But for Pap, Abram, Edward, and others, this wasn't just about getting land or farming. This was about getting what Jake Simmons Sr. and his family had: a geographic claim to start on the path toward Black nationalism—the concerted effort to unify identity for Black people, even in the form of a separate Black nation. Former enslaved Blacks who left the South, people like Abram and Edward who left city living, and those who made their way back like Pap came for a dream.

Most of the six hundred in Nicodemus were recently freed or

never-enslaved Blacks who had left for greener pastures beyond the
grip of white supremacy. Others had left states and cities along the
Mississippi River and landed throughout Kansas, Oklahoma, and
even as far west as Colorado. More than forty thousand Blacks arrived in Kansas alone during this period.

They were fleeing the nightmare that white America had created.
Remember that Andrew Johnson, a Southerner, didn't take up the
causes of enfranchisement and protection of new Black voters. He
stood by as Black Codes proliferated throughout the South, and the
South's lessons served as inspiration for Creek leaders like Samuel
Checote, who vied for similar codes in the Creek Nation. This
uncertainty led to the emergence of Black Codes, which Douglas
Blackmon details in his book *Slavery by Another Name*—arguing
that the Codes, among other things, were a type of reenslavement.
These actions by racist white people made life untenable for thousands of Black people. So these families left where they lived and
moved west to become Exodusters.

Imagine how tired these Exodusters must have been. Years of
war and bloodshed and more than two centuries of racial terror.
The only hope to ensure that the dream of freedom wouldn't become a nightmare was to leave your home. Because slavery by many
other names wasn't necessarily over.

Eventually, Abram and Edward made their way to Nicodemus.

They were able to show that they were men of "good moral character," which was enough to pass the equivalent of the bar in Kansas
and to license both of them as lawyers. They sold their services as
such, even though they had never attended a day of law school or set
foot in a courtroom. Abram's knowledge of French and Latin allowed him to pass as a well-educated Negro who wielded the power

of the quill. And with their land and location agency in full swing, they soon played pivotal roles in brokering land deals under the firm name Hall & McCabe: Locators and Land Agents.

Once they settled in Nicodemus, Abram got to writing and reporting, while Edward entered politics in a state that was less than twenty years old and in a settlement that hadn't yet reached the first anniversary of its founding. Abram started his newspaper, this time not as the *Chicago Citizen* but as *The Colored Citizen*. After a time helping to organize Nicodemus within Graham County, Abram moved on to St. Louis. Edward stayed and doubled down on his political career as a dream began to take shape.

Edward's rapid rise in politics mirrored his similar ascent in business. He thought that this emerging Black life would have its best chance through populating places that would welcome (or not immediately eschew) Black settlers.

By 1878, Edward was selected to serve as secretary of Nicodemus at the small town's first anniversary. Two years later, his time as a clerk on Wall Street came in handy as he parlayed his growing stature in the community to become Graham County clerk from Nicodemus.

At the same time, state politics in Kansas and throughout the Reconstruction South and Midwest were changing. Figuring out what role the eventual ninety-six thousand Black Exodusters in Kansas would play meant that Edward's time had come. He quickly became an increasingly important political force in the state. The Republican Party was anchored in part at the time by Samuel Pomeroy, the same senator who protected the cause of Cow Tom and the rest of the Black Creek when President Johnson and his allies sought to strip Black people of opportunities. Edward became a delegate-at-large from Kansas to the 1880 Republican convention in Chicago that nominated James Garfield. He had to navigate the intricacies of a radicalizing Republican Party. Doing so meant temporarily allying with conservative factions even if it made him the target of members of the State Convention of Colored Men in April 1880, who called him a "sellout" for working with the conservatives. But in Edward's opinion, "[I] strove hard, single-handed, to secure a representation for my race, but without avail." His politicking, however, reached its pinnacle when he was elected Kansas state auditor and was reelected two years later.

But his political achievements always came second to his dreams of Black nationalism, especially when he caught, as Charlotte Hinger put it, "Oklahoma Fever."

Across the country, word had gotten out that opportunity was bursting in Oklahoma. And reports were circulating that Blacks had a chance to make their own way there.

But Edward, like Jake Sr., wasn't interested in just a chance. He was looking to place roots and call something his and his people's own. Throughout Kansas, "Oklahoma clubs" were forming and meeting in secret to plan a way out. The angst fueled by the proliferation of racism through Black Codes had found its way to the Exodusters, who realized it was time to leave the South. Black newspapers carried stories of the advisability of leaving the South, as well as accounts of settlers who were waiting on the borders of Oklahoma territory for free land. By 1910, *The Topeka Plaindealer* reported that "a large percentage of the negro population on the eastern side of the state [had] rich allotments from their Indian citizenship."

Immigration societies popped up in Topeka, and W. L. Eagleson, one of the heads of the Oklahoma Emigration Association, addressed Blacks in the South with a proposition that sounded appealing for thousands of Black folks: "There never was a more favorable time than now for you to secure good homes in a land where you will be free and your rights respected. Oklahoma is now open for settlement."

To Eagleson, Oklahoma represented the very "best state in the union" because Blacks could create opportunities for themselves. He extolled the topography and land of this Eden: "The soil is rich, the climate favorable, water abundant and there is plenty of timber." And he compelled them, as James Baldwin encouraged readers to do in *Just above My Head*, to begin again: "Make a new start. Give yourselves and children new chances in a new land, where you will not be molested and where you will be able to think and vote as you please." He pulled on the heartstrings of parents to consider that "by settling [in Oklahoma] you will help open up new avenues of industry, your boys and girls will learn trades and thus be able to do business as other people. Five hundred of the best colored citizens of Topeka have gone there within the last month. They send back word for others to come on, there is room for many more." Eagleson and Edward believed that there was more just beyond the reaches of Kansas's southern border—just over a two and a half days' march from Topeka.

Eagleson and McCabe assumed that there would be twenty thousand Black immigrants from Kansas ready to move into Oklahoma. Groups formed quickly, such as the First Colored Real Estate Homestead and Emigration Association of the State of Kansas, which provided help for Blacks hoping to settle in the great West of Oklahoma. A year later, the *American Citizen* newspaper published a piece that detailed the intricacies of trying to build an all-Black community in Oklahoma. Edward McCabe became known as a leader of these efforts; his work was chronicled by A. G. Stacey: "While not generally known, and certainly never advertised in the press, there is a secret political society in existence, membership in which can be obtained only by those of Negro blood. Last year there was organized by a little band of Negroes in Graham county [where Nicodemus, Edward's adopted hometown, is located] the first Grand Independent Brotherhood, which is based upon the principles of Negro advancement, mentally and morally, and the future control of Oklahoma whenever it shall become a state. . . . An auxiliary society, called an 'immigration society,' was formed, which undertook the work of reaching the Negroes of the south to hasten their movement to the promise [*sic*] land."

The promised land would've never been reached without its then-Moses and his guides, Joshua and Caleb. It took the willing courage of Joshua and Caleb to look beyond the borders to determine whether moving forward was worthwhile. According to Stacey, the Joshuas and Calebs of their day scouted and "worked only in Arkansas and Mississippi where the results were most marked." But they soon realized that "there was a scarcity of labor in those states" that wasn't the case in Indian Territory. According to Stacey, the "Negro settlement began to appear and grow as if by magic. Near Purcell a large one was founded; on the East Canadian two Negro settlements founded; west of Kingfisher others were commenced and grew so rapidly that they were towns before the neighboring whites realized what was being done."

By that point, Stacey estimated that "Shawnee county has alone furnished 3,000 Negroes all of whom had money. Chautauqua,

Montgomery, Wyandotte, and Leavenworth counties have sent at least 4,000 more, while from other counties in the state, headed by Graham, the original home of the society, have gone fully 3,000 more, making 10,000 from Kansas alone."

And it wasn't just Kansans making their way to Indian Territory. Stacey said that "the auxiliary immigration society has been to add some 12,000 Negroes from Arkansas and Mississippi, making in all about 22,000 Negroes in the territory, which number the brotherhood is bending every energy to make 50,000 before September 1."

The optimism and the demand that came with it for what awaited Black folks in Indian Territory wasn't shared universally. Some thought Oklahoma was a well-promoted pipe dream: "In God we trusted. In Oklahoma we busted," as one writer wrote in the *Leavenworth Advocate*. Others viewed the push to move Black life to Oklahoma and to make Oklahoma an all-Black state as becoming more far-fetched; white and Black writers called it a plan hatched by those who thought they could profit the most: "speculators, land grabbers, and office seekers." A white newspaper, *The Topeka Capital*, alleged that Black people weren't wise enough to realize that they were about to become victims.

Despite the naysaying, many blacks did move to Oklahoma, in part because the calls in Black newspapers for Black self-determination rang loudly, as did the voice of O. L. Garrett's letter published in the Detroit *Plaindealer* on November 15, 1889:

> We are here first as American citizens; we are here because
> as such we have the right to be here to better our condition
> and if permitted to prove beyond question that we possess
> the qualifications of earnest, thrifty, capable and law abiding

citizens—equal, in fact to the more favored race in con-
ducting if necessary the affairs of a State without jars or
friction to anyone who may cast their lot with us, of any
race or nationality. . . . You are not wanted in the South.
Then embrace this, perhaps your last opportunity to get
lands for yourselves and families.

As you can imagine, Black people moving onto land where there
were already thousands of Black members of the Five Tribes living
freely in Oklahoma did not sit well with the whites who sought to
make this land theirs.

Sooners, the white settlers who came to Oklahoma during the
Land Rush to take what the Five Tribes had been promised would
never be taken away, were sparked with the fear that Black people
moving into Oklahoma meant less for them. Soon Ku Klux Klan
members, many of whom were also part of this collection of so-
called Sooners, raided Black families and developing communities.
Edward McCabe was caught up in this racist violence. According
to the Louisiana newspaper *The Daily Picayune*, "The nearest approach to bloodshed occurred when ex-auditor McCabe of Kansas,
the founder of the negro colony at Langston, started for Guthrie
through Iowa lands. He was met by three men, who ordered him to
go back whence he came. He declined and they opened fire on him.
One shot struck the [pommel] of his saddle, and being unharmed, he
fled back to Langston, and from there came to Guthrie."

It eventually dawned on Edward that despite his dreams of an
all-Black state and his promise that there'd be 100,000 Black people
in Indian Territory, America might not be ready to accommodate

free and prosperous Black people on land coveted by white settlers who felt entitled to it.

Edward's dream of an all-Black state shrank to a city: Langston, which was named after Black congressman John Mercer Langston and is home today to Oklahoma's one historically Black college, Langston University. The town became known as "The Only Distinctly Negro City in America," even though the Creeks had three main Black towns already and more districts in larger cities like Muskogee.

But even Edward's minimized dream of an all-Black city was met by opposition—including from white members of his own Republican Party. White Republicans called him a "pushahead" because in their eyes Edward had become too big for his britches, trying to become governor of the territory.

It all came to a head when Edward spoke at the Republican county convention in 1892. In the middle of telling Blacks that the Republican Party had let them down and that their dream had been deferred once again, he was ruled out of order by white members of the Republican Party. McCabe leaned on his Black colleagues to make an impassioned stance in support, climbing back onto the stage to deride the party he had worked to build both in Kansas and in Oklahoma.

As a result, Black delegates left the Republican Party and their political leverage ended with it, as did their chances of convincing the white status quo that an all-Black state could be achieved.

Edward left Oklahoma for several years to work in Washington, D.C., but he still strove for a Blacker Oklahoma, lobbying President Benjamin Harrison to be appointed territory governor. By 1897 he returned to Oklahoma as deputy auditor of Oklahoma Territory, a post he held until 1907 when Oklahoma became a state. And when Oklahoma decided to pass its own Jim Crow laws, McCabe moved back to Chicago, without a Black state having been created.

Edward McCabe never got to live his dream, because his dream had not one trapping of citizenship that tied him to the land. In fact, he died a pauper. Even Jake Simmons Sr. got the chance to live that dream a little bit longer than Edward could have ever imagined, because Jake and his family were part of the land.

JAKE SIMMONS and the rest of the Black Creeks could've tried to live inside a vacuum, shielded from a world that told Black people that they weren't worthy of respect. But his family's living their dreams was scaring others and crafting nightmares.

In 1898, *The Oklahoma City Times* published a story that was then carried by other Oklahoma newspapers, and its publication seemed a warning—an indication of things to come, a near cautionary tale. Its phrasing didn't sound dissimilar from what one might hear today at rallies for people who mean Black people no good. The writer wrote, "In certain parts of the former Indian Territory, the Negro-Creek is a thing to be dreaded. [Just] such a combination of aboriginal cruelty and ferocity can be found perhaps nowhere on earth except in the new state of Oklahoma." Without evidence, the writer accused what he called the "Negro Creek" of having a "ferocious disposition" and alleged that they hid under a "very thin veneer of civilization," likening them to Frankenstein's monster. And the name-calling came with a biblical threat the writer alleged would give "the saner citizens some comfort": "He that taketh up the sword shall perish by the sword."

The writer tried to rewrite history with all the racist language he could muster, saying that the "half-romantic" origins of the "Negro Creek" stemmed from the tendencies of the Creek to be runaway slaves. These runaway slaves hid themselves in the brakes of the Alabama country and became as wild and savage as their Indian protectors with one difference: the negro was "several times as intelligent, as resourceful and as courageous as the Indian." The writer was trying to convince readers that Jake Simmons Sr., his family, and all others like him were not only wild and savage but also intelligent about their savagery—"the most dangerous man on the American continent today."

It was the mixing of Native blood and African blood that concerned the writer most, saying that the Indian "is an assassin who will himself stand the stake and the knife without a whimper, but beyond this his ratio of courage does not go. It was only when the negro blood became mixed with that of the Indian that the barbarity of both races showed up in its true colors."

According to this writer, it was the duty of the white citizen to figure out what to do with the "Negro Creek." And no matter how great and expansive the lived dreams of Jake Simmons Sr. and his family might have been, their fate and that of other "Negro Creek" people in the hand of the "white citizen" seemed predetermined in the concluding sentence of the article:

"The day of the Negro-Creek is indeed done."

CHAPTER 11

YOU'LL KNOW HIM
BY HIS FRUIT

Therefore, by their fruits you will know them.

MATTHEW 7:16

I n 1957, the Black sociologist E. Franklin Frazier published a book
  about the Black middle class, *The Black Bourgeoisie*. In it, he
  explored the notion that business success and capitalism could
ever produce racial equality in America. It's not an unfamiliar argument: Black people, like other groups on society's margins, have tried
to do what white America has demanded of them to be accepted,
only to realize that it's futile.

"The Black bourgeoisie, who have striven to mold themselves in the image of the white man, have not been able to escape from the mark of racial inferiority," Frazier wrote.

And it's true. It's the reason that I fled Oklahoma for Harvard and Oxford—stocking up on every measure of the bourgeoisie fervor I could. But I still get pulled over by the police seemingly wherever I drive, I still get told that I'm "less than" by society, and I still inspire white women to clutch their purses closer when I walk by.

Jake Simmons and his son, Jake Simmons Jr., prosperous though they were, didn't try to meet some bar of respectability. Their goal was to plant roots in a place that for a time seemed outside the reaches of white supremacy.

PERHAPS THE BEST WAY to tell the story of Jake Simmons Jr. is to start where his story ends.

Jonathan Greenberg, who was a business writer for *Forbes*, wrote a book about him and recounted that on the day Jake Jr. died in 1981 in his hometown of Muskogee, the city hall and courts closed in his honor. Legendary Oklahoma Democratic governor George Nigh made his way to Muskogee to eulogize Jake Jr., and hundreds of others came from as far away as Ghana to pay their respects at Ward Chapel African Methodist Episcopal Church, right off Denison Street in downtown Muskogee. Jake Jr. had spent years serving on its board and channeled much of his philanthropy through the church and its seminary, Shorter College.

Why would a Black man in Oklahoma whom you've likely never heard of garner such a diverse crowd at his funeral? Why would

Jake Simmons Jr. be the man whom Muskogee—a town whose population at the time was less than 11 percent Black—honored by closing its schools and city government buildings on the day of his funeral?

The answer is simple: Jake Simmons Jr. was a Black man who was born on a springboard that came with his citizenship in the Creek Nation. His citizenship gave him land. And that land gave him a glimpse of what it takes to make it in America.

IN 1982, Jonathan Greenberg was given an assignment whose initial mandate came straight from the top: "Compile a ranking of the wealthiest people in America, the first-ever Forbes 400." Malcolm Forbes, the publisher of the magazine, had told Greenberg's editor, Jim Michaels, not just to compile the list from government data, but to try to dig into information about people's private holdings and equities. Greenberg abandoned the northeast orbit of business journalism anchored by *Forbes* to, as described in a retelling of the list's birth in an article written by Chase Peterson-Withorn, "hit Dallas, Houston and Midland in search of America's great oil fortunes, [travel] from old-money Boston to the nascent Silicon Valley tech scene and [make] stops in Atlanta, Detroit, Chicago, Tulsa and dozens of other cities."

In his travels, Greenberg stopped in Oklahoma to find high-networth individuals for the list without tipping them off to the magazine's intent. Greenberg met with Taft Welch, chairman of the board of the Western National Bank in Oklahoma, to find people in Oklahoma who might be candidates for the list of the four hundred richest Americans. Before Greenberg could go into detail, Welch scolded him, saying, "You're missin' Jake Simmons from Muskogee. The colored fella who put Phillips into Africa. He's a born raider worth more than any of the names you got heah!"

Though Jake Jr.'s net worth couldn't be calculated by Greenberg or the *Forbes* team, it was clear he was a man to pay attention to.

IN 1890, Robert Porter and Carroll Wright administered a Department of the Interior census of the Five Nations. "Negro Indians, especially in the Creek Nation, can be found in abundance," they wrote. They commented on the vibrancy of the Five Nations but especially focused on the uniqueness of the Creek Nation. "The Creek Nation is an alert and active one," they wrote, "which is largely due to the negro element which fairly controls it. The negroes are among the most earnest workers in The Five Tribes. The Creek Nation affords the best example of negro progress. The principal chief, 'virtually a negro,' comes of a famous family in Creek annals and who famous Creek contemporary poet Alex Posey accused of looking more 'Negro than white.'"

Porter and Wright didn't just imagine this world; they witnessed this Black success in the Creek Nation with their own eyes. They saw Blacks like Jake Simmons Sr. embody Black accomplishment and progress.

Jake Simmons's economic and business successes were real, and they were built on the foundation of Creek citizenship. And it was Creek citizenship that made Porter and Wright describe these Black Creeks with the loaded term "virtually negroes." These virtual negroes were chronicled in *The Topeka Plaindealer* in 1910: "A large percentage of the negro population on the eastern side of the state [had] rich allotments from their Indian citizenship."

Jake Jr. grew up at the height of this Black abundance. His father was one of the most successful Black ranchers of the time and dreamed that his children, especially his sons, would continue his tradition of ranching. His father had established his dominance in ranching on the outer borders of Haskell, Oklahoma, near Muskogee. When Jake Jr. was a child, the Muskogee City Council had Black councillors, a concept unheard of in a town that wasn't explicitly an "all-Black town." Its Blackness and its Creekness created opportunities when so many other Black Americans had limited chances for success. In the words of the Black editor of *The Muskogee Cimeter*, William Twine, "The Indian Territory is the last stand the Negro of America can make as a pioneer and we propose to let it go down in history that the stand was made here and that the loyal members of the race stood as a stone wall for justice and right and at all times were loyal to their race, their country and their God. . . . We will show to the world that the Negro pioneers of the West are breaking the way for posterity to follow and that in the early years of the 20th century to live under the wings of the American eagle and under the shining folds of the star spangled banner will live in peace."

To some extent, the town of Muskogee contained vibrant Black life. The Simmons family would go into town to buy shoes, clothes, and odds and ends—often from Black shop owners. They would take their horses to compete at county fairs. They'd get together with other Black kids, often of other Black Creeks, who lived on their

Black-owned plots, to enjoy their Black abundance on their own Black terms.

At this time early in the twentieth century, Black life on the eastern side of Indian Territory was inextricably tied to that of the Creek Nation. Nearly 37 percent of the Creek Nation was made up of Black people, living on more than one million acres. The representation of Black Creeks in terms of land was far more pronounced than that of the Blacks in the other Nations, who all together had one million acres. Land ownership, which had been a dream of Edward McCabe, was a reality for Jake Simmons and his children.

As Greenberg wrote in *Forbes*: "Blacks in the Creek Nation were born lucky: they received not just forty acres, but a 160-acre 'freehold.' This may not have transformed the entire world, but it certainly altered the world of Jake Jr.'s youth." Why? Because Jake was born before the March 4, 1907, cutoff, he was entitled to 160 acres of land specifically because he was Creek. The promise of 40 acres and a mule was left unfulfilled for millions of Black families, but for Jake—thanks to his forebears' negotiating skills—it was his birthright. And with land ownership came the means of controlling production. No wonder Booker T. Washington found the success and wealth of the Simmons family attractive enough to recruit young Jake to attend the Tuskegee Institute.

In contrast, white people who came to Oklahoma for a chance to take the land that belonged to Blacks and Native Americans had different ideas. They'd come from states where they were used to Blacks taking a back seat to white lives and livelihood. They were used to the entitlement that came from their own skin color. But once they entered the eastern part of Oklahoma, they had to adjust to the anomaly of successful Black folk.

For Black Creeks, living presented a problem for white supremacists. In addition to barring Blacks from traveling in the same train
cars as whites, Haskell and his legislative peers went further. They
passed anti-miscegenation laws preventing Blacks from marrying Native Americans, though whites could continue marrying into Native
American families.

By 1910, Democrats in Congress ripped from Blacks, Creek or not,
the right to vote by grandfathering an amendment to the Constitution
that limited voting eligibility to those who were allowed to vote before January 1, 1866, a date that barred virtually every Black man in
America. And if you were lucky enough to be eligible to vote as a
Black person, you'd have to pass a literacy test, which no white voter
was subjected to.

IN THE EARLY TWENTIETH CENTURY, Oklahoma was booming. Between 1907 and 1930, Oklahoma vied with California for
the title of the top oil-producing state. When Jake Simmons Jr. was
ten, his father asked all of his sons what they wanted to be when
they grew up. Jake's brothers aspired to be farmers, ranchers, and
cowboys. Jake Jr. wanted to be an oilman. It was a dream he'd ful-
fill.

Twenty-one miles from Jake Jr.'s house lived a woman named Ida
Glenn. Jake Jr. would've heard about "Ida Glenn Number One."

In Tulsa County, there was a small plot of land that was allotted
to Robert and Ida Glenn, two Black Creek citizens. It sat for years
without anyone understanding what was beneath it. But two enterprising wildcatters, aspiring oilmen, obtained a lease on the allotment provided to Mrs. Glenn. By 1904, Ida and her husband received

a measly $45, or $1,300 today, to lease the land long enough to drill for oil on it. Ida and Robert retained one eighth of the proceeds from whatever oil would be found.

And find oil the oil tycoons did. For years, seventy-five to eighty-five barrels of good black gold were drilled from a well on that land every day. Though the oil field was eventually abandoned in the 1960s, over the course of its life it produced 340 million barrels of oil. The town that started with twelve families—the Black Creek family of the Glenns being among them—soon jumped in population and was renamed Glenpool after this enterprising Black couple. Black Oklahomans, and especially Black Creek landowners, were part of a new type of businesspeople: landowners who became oilmen.

Jake Jr. wanted to be one of those Black Oklahomans.

While he knew at age ten that life on the ranch was not for him, Jake Jr. did work on his father's land. He fed cows, cleaned out dung, and more. Eventually he took Booker T. Washington's offer to study at the Tuskegee Institute. Jake would start a year younger than the average student; spend five years in Tuskegee, Alabama; graduate; and then migrate north to work in a Ford plant.

Before he could build a life in Detroit, however, opportunity sprang from the ground in the form of oil on land he owned. Jake Sr. contacted his son to tell him that his land had oil under it. His Creek identity, fought for and protected for generations by his forebears, made his dream of becoming an oilman a reality.

After he returned to Oklahoma, Jake Jr. married Eva Flowers, whose parents also were Creek and who also owned Creek land for which they received oil royalties. He didn't need to live on his land to administer it. But he was light on cash, so instead of gambling what little money he had to drill for more oil, Jake Jr. became a broker. Many people—Black Creeks and non-Black Creeks—worked with Jake Jr. to broker deals between wildcatters. He started first with his parents' land. He'd get royalties from the renters and companies who drilled oil on the land, and his family and his eventual clients would collect revenue on one eighth of the oil found.

He didn't stop there. He created a real estate company to help identify and prospect land, negotiate land deals, offer options on lands for mineral rights, and at times estimate and sell farmland. He mastered swap options, ownership titles, deeds, and nearly every aspect of the transaction process. He became so adept that he was able to strike deals with wealthy white oilmen who were willing to overlook the color of his skin for the money that Jake Jr. would make them. To the white oilmen of the time, greed had no race.

In 1929 the Great Depression hit. But it hit more lightly for Jake Jr. precisely because he wasn't like others in America who faced economic ruin.

Capital dried up quickly and so did the business of drilling, which depended on capital. As such, the oil lease business that Jake Jr. used to build his rapid wealth was reduced to almost nothing. But because the Simmons land (and that of his wife) was owned outright and the family kept farm animals, Jake Jr. and his family avoided the twin scourges of poverty and hunger that plagued millions of others. He had more than enough land to sell to continue generating revenue.

But the benefits of his Creek identity didn't stop there. He sold land to wealthy Black Texans just as many Black Texans were experiencing racial terror in Texas. He'd show them the all-Black towns and the highly concentrated parts of Black Muskogee, where he owned significant property. He lured them by telling them of the well-to-do Black families who owned shops and land as far as the eye could see, and he could speak of the prosperous lives of Black families who created for themselves enclaves just slightly more distant from the haunt of racism than parts of Texas.

As a Black man, Jake was able to attract the attention of Black Texans who distrusted white brokers. And as a Creek man, he could leverage his identity's deep roots in the land. He was doubly blessed—the blessing and fortune unearned by him but warranted by birthright.

These opportunities carried him and his family through the Great Depression. But to prosper, Jake Jr. had to go farther, striking deals not just in Oklahoma but throughout East Texas, which at that time was a hotbed of racial violence. At the time, Frank Phillips, founder of what is now ConocoPhillips, made some of his first big deals working in Indian Territory with the Osage Nation. So Jake Jr. leveraged his Blackness and his Creek identity to work with Phillips as his broker. And broker deals and sell oil leases he did. He went on to work with the founders of Sinclair Oil, Skelly Oil, and Spartan Aircraft Company, as well as Texaco and other companies. Often they would front Jake the money to acquire large plats of land that he would then sell and lease to others.

While Creek land was his home base, he expanded across Oklahoma, East Texas, Arkansas, Louisiana, and Kansas. With his business prowess and a claim to the land that predated Oklahoma becoming a state, Jake Jr. was, more than most Black people, able to have a voice on topics and issues and speak his mind.

He advised governors on juvenile detention centers and state mental facilities reserved for Black people. He chaired the Oklahoma chapter of the National Association for the Advancement of Colored People. He helped finance constitutional challenges to the segregation practiced in the state and sued the district attorney of Muskogee, the town's mayor, and the state board of education for unfairly limiting educational benefits for Black children. And for his efforts, he earned not only a date in the U.S. Supreme Court for a case that bore his family name—*Simmons v. Muskogee Board of Education*—but also a nickname: "radical troublemaker." Though his reputation among local and state political leaders soured, no one could deny Jake Jr. his seat at the table, because the table was on his people's land. Though *Simmons v. Muskogee Board of Education* was dismissed by the Court, it canonized Jake Jr. as a fixture of Black liberation in Oklahoma.

His prowess extended beyond the United States. He brokered oil deals in Ghana, Nigeria, and Liberia. But his greatest achievements weren't medals from African heads of state or successful negotiations with government leaders. His greatest achievement was his legacy. Leadership runs in the family. As his niece Johnnie Mae put it, "We got big government leaders, oilmen, teachers, postmasters, you name it! We got 'em all!"

AS A CHILD I never considered what it would look like if Black folks had a leg up from birth, one that predated a white person giving them any support. Until I learned about Jake Simmons Jr. and the rest of the Simmons family, I never considered what it meant to be part of a family in which the sacrifices your ancestors made paid dividends for you. My reading of American history told me that Black people went from slavery to Jim Crow to another kind of slavery, one behind bars thanks to government policies like the war on drugs.

Jake Simmons Jr. and his life provided the answer to the question I've asked myself for too long: What if Black people's assertion of mattering didn't depend on what society—or more precisely, white people—had to say? What would it look like for the children of trailblazing Black people not shackled by slavery, Jim Crow, the war on drugs, and even our lives today?

Jake's four children had that sense of self. Don Simmons went on to run his father's company, the Simmons Royalty Company, and continued to run the company late into his life. Kenneth attended Harvard and taught for decades at Berkeley. Blanche pursued a career in social work throughout the Southwest. And his namesake, Jake Simmons III, eventually joined the Kennedy administration and would become an undersecretary of the Interior Department during the first Reagan administration and a member of the Interstate Commerce Commission in the 1980s and 1990s.

The Simmons family isn't necessarily the blueprint for what all Black success should look like, but by examining their start, which was accelerated by full citizenship in the Creek Nation, we can imagine ways that Black life could flourish in America if they received such support.

I didn't have to go far to see what Black success looked like. I had to look just a few miles south of my hometown to capture a glimpse of the story of a Black family named Simmons, whose citizenship was Creek, and who had an ancestor known as Cow Tom.

Two years before Jake Jr.'s funeral in 1979, his and his family's claim to citizenship in the Creek Nation came to an end—upending his family's long-standing residence in a Nation that crafted citizenship and identity that his family had helped forge.

CHAPTER 12

JOHNNIE MAE STOPPED
GETTING MAIL

It's just who I was.

JOHNNIE MAE AUSTIN

Plastered across the June 15, 1997, edition of the *Tulsa World* was the headline "Creek Nation to Honor Longtime Chief." Datelined Okmulgee, the story said that unlike "other Indian leaders [who] are involved in controversy and scandals," the longtime chief being honored was not. His name was Claude Cox and he had led the Creek Nation for twenty years. Among his accomplishments listed, the one the article focused on was that he "brought Indian gaming to Oklahoma," which was an economic boon for the state.

The piece quoted Cox recalling his first days in office: "There was me, a desk, and I got an advisory board of seven people. We ran this place the best we could." When he became chief, the Creek

Nation's annual budget was $20,000. When he left two decades later, the Nation had an operating budget of $13 million and employed "1,000 in 45 facilities in eight Oklahoma counties." Cox indisputably set the Nation on a path of long-term growth. The article reported the Creek Nation's status as of 1997: "The tribe has a $94 million annual budget—including health, housing and gaming enterprises—and employs 2,200 people in 80 facilities." Cox's support of gaming made gambling and gaming an economic engine for the Creek and the state of Oklahoma. Oklahoma allowed the Creeks to open "a 39-bed hospital in Okemah, [build] housing projects (which now total more than 2,000 units) and [institute] educational programs."

CLAUDE COX DID what no Creek chief had ever done and what other leaders wish they could do: be reelected so often that your political prowess is unquestioned and your legacy secured.

Remembering heroes is tricky because readers of history who live in the shadows of history's legacy have to make judgment calls about how much of the bad about these figures we will tolerate in the name of remembering the good. Today we decry Mount Rushmore not only because it is carved out of the sacred mountain range of the Lakota, but because of the men whose faces are etched into it. President George Washington, who though he founded this country also earned the nickname Conotocaurius—Town Destroyer—for his uncivil attempts to "civilize" and "solve" the so-called Indian Problem. Or Theodore Roosevelt, who may have protected wildlife and public lands by creating the U.S. Forest Service and five national parks, but who said of the Indian, "I don't go so far as to think that the only good Indians are the dead Indians, but I believe nine out of every 10 are." We have these debates about what great men and great women throughout history have done and we memorialize them, carefully trying to pick out what will and will not be remembered. Because remembering history tells us far more about who we are and who we aspire to be.

Remembering Claude Cox, a truly great Creek chief, and both his intentional acts and their unintended consequences tells us a great deal about what the world thinks of Black lives, especially the life of a Black Creek woman with a quiet voice and a loving temperament named Johnnie Mae Austin, who just stopped getting her mail.

IT WASN'T ONLY JAKE SIMMONS SR.'S immediate family that benefited from his success. In addition to his ten biological children, Jake Sr. helped raise four "outside kids," some "destitute adopted boys, and a variety of other relatives," according to Jake Simmons Jr.'s biographer. One of those relatives was Johnnie Mae Austin, the daughter of Jake's brother John.

When Johnnie Mae was born in 1932 on Creek land, the Creek Nation was going through radical change—change that altered Johnnie Mae's chances of claiming Creek citizenship. Her identity as a citizen of the Creek Nation has become intricately tied to the political success of Claude Cox. Austin's identity and her eventual exclusion from the Creek Nation were the collateral damage of Cox's march to make the Creek more independent.

One of the truths of American history is that white men have been telling people who are not white men who they are and who they can be. It's why racist policies have persisted and it's fundamentally why the controversy between the Creek Nation and its former Black citizens still brews.

After the Dawes Commission reallocated Native lands, some people had access to good lands while others—many others, especially those who were Creek citizens—were left with land that was unsuitable either for farming and ranching or for wildcatting. With nearly 100 million acres of the Creek Nation's land taken by the federal government, life got much harder for many Creeks, even if it didn't necessarily for the enterprising work of Jake Simmons, father and son.

In 1928, the Rockefeller Foundation funded the Institute for Government Research (IGR), the predecessor to what is now the Brookings Institution, to compile what became an 847-page report about what life was like for American Indians. Named for the erudite bureaucrat and report writer Lewis Meriam, the Meriam Report revealed the extreme poverty and devastation that Native people lived in, and it explicitly blamed the Dawes Commission, which had repatriated land the U.S. government said it would never touch, and the Curtis Act, which decimated tribal governments. It took nearly fifty years for those in the U.S. government to realize just how bad life had gotten for these Nations.

The report found that at the time, in 1928, the average life expectancy of an American Indian was 44 years; the average life expectancy of an average American was 55.6 years. The average income for an American household was $1,407; the study found that the average annual per capita income was $100 for America's Indigenous population.

These facts set down for anyone to see the perilous lives of people in America who are not white. Finally, the U.S. government had to reckon with the devastation it had caused.

Six years after the Meriam Report was released, Franklin Delano Roosevelt's commissioner of Indian affairs, John Collier, used the report to reverse decades of bad federal policy, but not by consulting the Nations and empowering them to set their own course. Instead, the Indian Reorganization Act of 1934 was passed, which allowed Indian tribes throughout the country to establish tribal governments under the pretext that the cultures of these Nations had something to teach the non-Indigenous population. The fact that the U.S. government had to re-legislate the power for Nations to do what any nation should have the right to do was only part of a larger problem.

Two years later, championed by a Democratic senator from Oklahoma, the Oklahoma Indian Welfare Act (OIWA) was passed. The OIWA stopped the allotment and loss of Indian lands, and reconstituted tribal governments.

On the surface these changes sound like progress. But often when you genuinely want to help, you ask those who need help how you can be most effective.

That did not happen here.

Instead, the U.S. government told the Nations that it was creating a governing organization called the Business Committee. This group limited the strength of internal democratic processes that had existed for generations in the Creek Nation. The separation of powers, which had existed in the Creek Nation before the United States tore apart its government, didn't find its way into the Business Committee structure. The executive, legislative, and judicial functions were all performed by the governing board.

Initially the Creeks said no to the OIWA form of governance. Without formal approval, the representatives of the forty-two Creek tribal towns, three of which were Black tribal towns, elected the

Nation's first principal chief in more than thirty years. Five years later, Harold Ickes, President Roosevelt's long-serving secretary of the interior, said to Roosevelt that he approved the Creek Convention as a legislative body, which acted like the Creek Council that Cow Tom and Legus Perryman had once known. In 1944, the Creek Nation's General Convention ratified a new constitution that merged the Business Committee's executive and legislative branches into the Creek Indian Council, which would govern the Creek Nation while not deviating too far from the Business Committee structure the OIWA provided.

Freedmen, Black Creeks, were left out of this vote. Black people like Johnnie Mae.

The Bureau of Indian Affairs (BIA) told the Creek Nation to reconstitute its government structure again. And it wasn't only the BIA that had problems with this. Chief John Davis, who came to power in 1951, rejected both the Creek Indian Council and the constitution this newer council produced.

Yet the U.S. government was inconsistent in advancing the independence and autonomy of the Creek. The BIA started to openly favor terminating the Creeks' tribal government, removing the principal chief role and cutting off the chance for Creeks to elect their leaders, the goal being to make the Nations more directly adherent to federal control and oversight.

On August 1, 1953, the House of Representatives passed a concurring resolution, House Concurrent Resolution 108, which was a formal statement that among other things announced the federal government's termination policy. Some tribes were terminated immediately and made citizens of the United States. But termination led to the end of aid, protections, and services, and in some cases reser-

vations. A total of 179 tribes were terminated. But perhaps most per-
niciously it called for the Department of the Interior to start finding
other tribes for termination quickly. It is why Dr. Dean Chavers
wrote in *Indian Country Today*, "The 1953 Termination or Bosone
Bill passed under the radar without any consultation with tribes, it
was possibly more devastating than the Dawes Act."

Remember what Angie Debo called American citizenship for the
Creek: a perilous gift. If the U.S. government granted "all of the rights
and prerogatives pertaining to American citizenship," then the promises and treaties that came before would no longer hold. Their citizenship as Americans—unasked for—nullified their Native governments,
their ways of life.

As the 1950s went on, the BIA started refusing Creeks the right
to elect a chief. Instead the BIA appointed the chiefs. The Creek
Tribal Council became an advisory committee that could only suggest ideas to the chief and the BIA; it could no longer govern. Since
that time, the council has served more as an advisory board than a
legislative body. So the Creek tribal government was often filled by
BIA appointees.

By 1964, trust in the chiefs appointed by the federal government
had plunged, even as money started to flow back into the Creek Nation as the United States began to pay small penalties for breaking
its numerous treaties. As a result, tribal towns began to take a more
prominent role in deciding what would happen in Creek life. While
the Creek Nation didn't get full autonomy, the towns within the
Creek Nation did.

As time went on, recommendations resurfaced both within and
outside the Creek Nation that they should govern themselves once
again, that limiting their opportunities would never result in the

success that the white men who ran the U.S. government were looking for.

On July 8, 1970, President Richard Nixon addressed Congress
to provide a Special Message to Congress on Indian Affairs. In his
address, he offered a new path forward for self-determination.
"This . . . must be the goal of any new national policy toward the
Indian people: to strengthen the Indian's sense of autonomy without
threatening his sense of community. We must assure the Indian that
he can assume control of his own life without being separated invol-
untarily from the tribal group. And we must make it clear that Indians can become independent of Federal control without being cut
off from Federal concern and Federal support."

One hundred eighty-five years after Benjamin Hawkins concluded
that there was an "Indian Problem" that needed a white man's solu-
tion, it took another president to realize that liberation and "help"
might be the worst solutions for Native people.

With this recognition came new legislation that transformed
Creek life. The same year as that speech, Congress passed the Principal Chiefs Act, which again allowed the Creek and other Nations
to elect their own chiefs.

Enter Chief Claude Cox, the longest-serving principal chief in the
history of the Creek Nation, who spelled the doom to Johnnie Mae's
mail.

CHIEF COX WOULD NOT HAVE BECOME a leader without the
Creek Nation getting its autonomy back. It turned to him in 1971.
Before this, Chief Cox worked until he was fifty-seven at the Public

Service Company of Oklahoma. According to historian Claudio Saunt, Cox "went as white before he became chief. Cox was a pole man for the rural electric company, and only white men could get these desirable jobs." After retiring from the company, he ran for chief of the Creeks and won. His task was clear: restore the Creek Nation, establish its system of governance, and generate revenue.

In every way, Cox followed through on these three tenets, though not without federal help. In 1975, after Nixon resigned the presidency, Congress passed the Indian Self-Determination and Education Assistance Act following the policy change he had called for five years earlier. The act moved the governing from unilateral control over Indigenous programs and services to empowering Indian Nations to create and design programs and services that responded to the needs of their people in their Nations—a practice that has persisted for more than forty years.

These changes allowed Claude Cox to begin building the foundation for what would become a large gambling revenue stream for the Nation, whose revenue established a hospital in Okemah and health and other social services for Creeks. Though the Creek Nation again could elect its own chiefs, for many of its other electoral and budgetary decisions, the Nation had to ask the federal government for approval. But standing in the way of any political victory is a political contest. Allen Harjo, another Creek leader, desperately wanted to become principal chief of the Creek Nation. He ran against Claude Cox in 1971 and 1975, and a key issue in the election was the National Council. Cox wanted to rewrite the Creek constitution to allow candidates to come from newly reconstituted districts as opposed to old towns, as they had originally. Harjo wanted to return to the old National Council and Creek representation as it had been laid out in the constitution that came after the treaty Cow Tom signed in 1866.

When Cox won reelection in 1975, Harjo challenged in federal district court the legal standing of the U.S. president to formally recognize only the Creek chief, not the Creek National Council. The decision of the U.S. District Court made it clear that tribal governments could administer nearly everything from housing to law enforcement, education, health, social service, and community development programs. The court had sided with Harjo, and in so doing, it removed whatever shackles the Creek Nation had in governing itself. The decision of the court empowered Cox and his officials to do something the Creek Nation hadn't done in more than a hundred years: rewrite and ratify a new constitution. But self-governance did not become equal governance for all Creek regardless of race. In fact, it killed it.

This new Creek constitution instituted something very different from the 1867 constitution. It spelled out Creek citizenship on grounds that it had never been defined as before.

JOHNNIE MAE RECALLED her great-uncle Jake Simmons, whom she called "Grandad," as being "Creek to the bone." She could recall him singing songs about the Creek Nation being her home. She, like other Black Creeks, grew up knowing that they were Creek. Johnnie grew up on Creek land in Oklahoma. Her grandparents taught her jokes and cuss words in Creek. She would travel from Haskell to Muskogee on her great-uncle's horse and buggy while Grandad told stories about what it meant to be Creek.

The first time I drove to Johnnie Mae's home in Tulsa I got lost trying to find it. But right around the bend of a steep turn, sitting in her walking chair, was Johnnie Mae Austin, dressed in sweatpants, a white shirt bedazzled with orange, red, purple, and green beads, and a pair of Croc-like shoes. She waved with one hand and with the other hand firmly gripped her large metal temperature-controlled cup.

She motioned for me to get out of the car and make my way into her home. Within seconds of being inside, I knew I had been transported back to being a young boy, when life looked a lot different for Black people.

Johnnie Mae's walls were covered with pictures. Of the schoolhouse she attended. Of her great-aunt Rose Simmons, who taught her to read. She pointed to the teacher's licenses of her family who had been teachers and principals of Black Creek schools—who were fully Black and fully Creek. She took out portraits of herself and her cousins. She showed me her cousins Don and JJ. She opened drawers and showed me the mail she'd received from the Creek Nation regularly over the years. Some of the letters alerted her to upcoming meetings. Others told her of elections within the Creek Nation. Some letters notified her of per capita payments for the settlement of lands or any money owed to Creeks for the countless offenses and treaty ruptures the U.S. government had committed. Some of those payments were like the one distributed by Commissioner Louis Bruce in 1972, which paid $4.9 million to the Creek Nation—equivalent to more than $31 million today.

For me, her house stood as a true expression of what it means to be fully Black and fully Creek.

Shaking her head as she looked at a picture of Jake Sr. and Rose on their land, she said, "He'd be devastated, my grandfather especially. Devastated." Devastated because Johnnie Mae, his grand-daughter, no longer has a home in the Creek Nation.

Johnnie grew up in Haskell, Oklahoma, on Jake Sr.'s two-thousand-acre ranch. She recalled how he "was all Creek all the time . . . Creek to the bone and so was my grandmother."

Yet they weren't Creek enough to pass as Creek, and it wasn't because they didn't have the documents to prove their lineage. No, Johnnie Mae's family became too Black to be Creek nearly thirty years before she was born.

Beginning in 1902, every Creek family or those who believed themselves to be part of the Nation had to re-enroll in the Nation. In order to enroll, each adult had to appear before a committee, usually of white men, and prove they were who they said they were. Their "Creekness" had to be validated by white men who had invented rigid categories that weren't consistent with Creek life: you were either "Freedman" or "by blood." Depending on which category a Black family fell into, if you were by blood, you were considered "purer" Creek, almost untainted by the perceived negative of being Black. If you were Freedman, it meant that you were a descendant of slaves. This was a name given all too often to Black Creeks, even if they were never descended from slaves. Before this time, being Freedman or by blood didn't matter to Black Creeks because they had always been and would remain Creek. Or so they thought.

Yet on March 13, 1902, Jake and Rose Simmons went from being Creek without asterisk, caveat, or exception to being Creek Freedman, a designation that forever tampered with the notion of identity without qualifiers. By becoming "Freedman," the Simmonses' legacies became inextricably linked with slavery.

Traditionally, Creek lineage is matrilineal. So Rose's deep and direct familial ties to Creek leadership—such as her grandfather, Cow Tom, a former chief—would have made her a guaranteed Creek on the "by blood" roll. As both Johnnie Mae and Damario recalled, Rose Simmons "handled all the business" of being Creek. When Dawes came, "[Jake Sr. and the rest of the family] could have been put on as a Creek by blood. But when they dealt with [Rose], she looked like an African. And it didn't matter then to be Creek or Freedmen," Damario told me. He continued, "That's how some of these families got split up" on the rolls.

Johnnie Mae said it simply and powerfully: "I think [the Creek Nation] just considered us Black Africans and that's it."

That distinction wouldn't matter except the Harjo decision empowered Chief Cox to bolster the independence of his Nation by diluting the citizenship value of Black Creeks. The very case that entitled Cox and the Creek Nation to experience true autonomy and independence from the United States also gave them the independence they needed to toss out their Black brothers and sisters.

AS MUCH AS CHIEF COX should be remembered as the chief whose tireless work ensured a more self-determining future for the Creek, we must consider all that he did over that time. Because of Claude Cox's twenty years as chief, the Creek Nation established the groundwork for becoming a leader in the casino and gambling industries. Jamie Floyd, a past principal chief of the Creek Nation, said in 2019 that "the Muscogee (Creek) Nation is thriving" and that the Creek Nation is "undoubtedly an important part of the greater economy." He's right: gaming revenue in the fourth quarter of 2018 alone came in at more than $25 million. And it goes beyond gaming.

An economic impact report by the Creek Nation found that "the Nation contributes more than $1.4 billion a year to the national economy, accounting for more than 10,000 jobs and paying $443 million in wages and benefits. And its economic impact on Oklahoma in 2017 alone reached $866 million." The Nation's compact with the state government of Oklahoma has provided millions in education funding for the broader student population in Oklahoma.

Not only did the economic prospects of the Creek improve under Chief Cox, but he also oversaw the return of the Creek Nation to Creek hands. When the court found in favor of the Creek Nation in *Harjo v. Kleppe*, Cox and his supporters rewrote the Creek constitution in a way that, in his eyes, reflected the actual concerns of the Creek. And to a great extent, the constitution did that. Cox's constitution divided the Creek government into three branches—legislative, executive, and judicial—with a cabinet with departments that oversaw aspects of Creek life. In making the Creek Nation their own again, the Creeks started a new chapter in their history of self-determination.

AT 9:15 A.M. on October 29, 1977, Chief Claude Cox welcomed the members of the council to the quarterly council meeting. After a prayer by Reverend Tony Hill in the native Creek language, the singing of a Creek hymn, and a few words from the speaker of the house and famed artist Solomon McCombs, the meeting started. Roll was taken by Ann Holder, the recording secretary.

After a few preliminaries, Claude Cox cemented the fate of Johnnie Mae and thousands of others like her. "After the selection of the Chief, I came in, and we tried to write up a Constitution," Cox said.

"There was about 25 people who had an input on that Constitution. We put it together where we thought it was feasible and in the best interests of the Creek Nation to make it a strong Creek Nation." He continued, but more strongly and in a more full-throated fashion, "When you go back to the old Constitution, you are licked before you start," Cox said, "because it doesn't talk about INDIANS, it talks about CITIZENS of the CREEK NATION."

Cox had done what his many forebears would not do: he bought into the overly simplistic view that race should determine one's access to citizenship. He embraced the notion that the Creek Nation had uniquely rejected decades before: that people couldn't be both Black and Creek. Cox codified this view because, as with his choice to pass as white to get the job at the Public Service Company of Oklahoma, he knew that being white had a currency in America that no measure of hard work by a marginalized person could buy. He used the anti-Indigenous tropes that had been used against his ancestors and leveraged it to separate the Black people who had called the Creek Nation home.

As the meeting went on, Cox doubled down on this perspective, which had been created by the white men and the white supremacy that Cox had made a political career of rebuffing: "There were more that was non-Indians or half-blood or less, who outnumbered the fullbloods, all of these totaled about 11,000, and there were only 18,000 on the entire Roll, so there was only 9,000 above one-half blood. That's the reason they lost control; the FULLBLOOD lost control. That's what we're fighting, this blood quantum, trying to get back and let the people control because under the old Constitution, you've lost before you ever started."

As Cox put it, "If we want to keep the INDIAN in control we've got to take a good look at this thing and get us a Constitution that will keep the Creek Indian in control."

In an instant, Cox did what the leaders of the Dawes Commission had been begging to do all along: use the tactics of racism and white supremacy to narrow Creek identity to a matter of race. There was no mention by Cox of the overrunning of Sooners—white men—onto Indian land just a few decades before. According to Dr. Daniel Littlefield of the Sequoyah National Resource Center, there were roughly three hundred thousand poor whites in Indian Territory, many of whom expected that Creek land would be theirs in the lead-up to Oklahoma becoming a state. Many of these whites married into or were adopted by the Creeks and were considered full-blood members. But Black people whose legacy predated these white Sooners were somehow too Black to be Creek.

As Littlefield explained it, within "Muskogee Creek leadership at that time, there was a strong element of 'we are a tribe of Indians.'" Creek citizenship now had a litmus test: you or your ancestors couldn't be Black, or at least noticeably Black, when the Dawes Commission was equipping the Creek Nation with notions that blood quantum could be determined by white men.

Cox got his way. In 1979, the Creek Nation adopted a new constitution and in Article III, Johnnie Mae and thousands of other Black Creeks lost their constitutional claim to their identity:

> Section 4. Full citizenship in the Muscogee (Creek) Nation shall be those persons and their lineal descendants whose blood quantum is one-quarter (¼) or more Muscogee (Creek) Indian, hereinafter referred to as those of full citizenship. All Muscogee (Creek) Indians by blood who are

less than one-quarter (¼) Muscogee (Creek) Indian by
blood shall be considered citizens and shall have all rights
and entitlement as members of the Muscogee (Creek) Nation except the right to hold office.

Johnnie Mae wasn't on the "by blood" roll, and with the stroke
of a pen she was no longer Creek. The mail she once treasured—the
notifications to vote; the news about the Nation; the offers of social, education, and health services—was gone. Johnnie Mae Austin
stopped getting mail when she stopped being Creek.

As for Cox, he maintained his hold on Creek leadership for almost eleven more years, helping to usher in increased autonomy and
self-determination for those Creek by blood.

Whether or not he tried, Cox couldn't avoid the allure of white
supremacy to determine citizenship in the Creek Nation, and he
couldn't avoid taking up the benefits and advantages that passing as
white, or at least not being labeled Black, can offer.

HISTORIAN CLAUDIO SAUNT has written that Creeks would ask
their neighbors, "Did you hear who's Estelusti?" which was Creek
for "black man." What became clear was that answering this question came with "embarrassing revelations [that] became so frequent
that Creeks soon began to joke about the subject," Saunt wrote. According to Saunt, Creeks would rush "friends and, as if they possessed a choice piece of gossip," ask with excitement, "Did you hear
who's not Estelusti?" Passing as not Black became identity currency.

Unlike Chief Claude Cox, who passed as not Black even though
he had traces of African ancestry in his blood, the Simmons family

couldn't. These distinctions were arbitrary, and opting in and out of them works only if you're not Black. In changing the Creek citizenship parameters to exclude those who were not on the "by blood" roll, Cox did the unforgivable. Not only did he banish countless Black Creeks from Creek membership, but he also exorcised part of himself: his own African ancestry.

His nephew Buddy Cox stated it bluntly to Saunt: "We owned some, we were some, and we slept with some."

An unnamed female officer of the Creek Nation who knew Buddy and Saunt remarked while looking at a picture that they all looked Black, but then in relief added, "Thank God for Claude slipping that Constitution past."

The officer, like Claude Cox, knew that being Black in America, even if in the Creek Nation, was marginalizing.

Perhaps to Claude Cox's possible chagrin, his nephew admitted gregariously to Saunt, "I'm Estelusti." In other words, he too has African ancestry. The female officer who thanked God for getting the Creek constitution passed that disenfranchised Black Creeks admitted the same, saying: "My family is part black, too. But I don't show it, do I?" Buddy Cox even rhetorically presented an idea about having African ancestry when he commented, "Don't we all?"

In seeming fear of being identified as too Black to be Creek, the officer replied, "Not me."

NEVER BEFORE HAD the delineation between "by blood" and "Freedmen" affected Creek citizenship or its accompanying rights. But with the 1979 decision to rewrite the constitution, Chief Cox created a more independent and autonomous Creek Nation while at the same time making it less Black, ignoring the long legacy of Black progress, and intentionally stamping out future opportunities for Black Creek descendants. As much good as Claude Cox did for the Creek Nation, we must balance that good with the fact that before she died Johnnie Mae Austin never got to reclaim the citizenship she so treasured.

PART II

WHO WE CAN BECOME

CHAPTER 13

BECOMING A SIMMONS

When I discover who I am, I'll be free.

RALPH ELLISON

One of the issues the Tulsa City Council met to discuss on Wednesday, March 13, 2019, was the city's Equality Indicators report. Piloted in Tulsa and a handful of other cities, the Equality Indicators tool was designed to measure inequalities for Tulsa's disadvantaged populations—in essence, to point out how the city's poor and communities of color were disadvantaged. As I watched the choppy, public-access live feed from fifteen hundred miles away, the worry, concern, and dissension that Tulsans felt about the inequity that had come to color the city of four hundred thousand shot through my laptop screen. Obun Ukuam, a then-new Tulsan who had moved from Ferguson, Missouri, just months earlier, said, "No matter what we're dealing with now, if we do not solve it and find a way to come together to address it, it will explode the way it did in Ferguson in 2014. It will explode in a way that is damaging to the city, damaging to the people, and damaging to the reputation of the city."

The report's findings were ugly. They showed that Black Tulsans were five times as likely as Hispanic Tulsans to have force used on them by police officers and that white Tulsans were half as likely to experience use of force by police compared with Black Tulsans. It confirmed what Black people and perhaps many non-Black people in the state already knew: that the state and the city address Black residents with more violence than comity, more animus and angst than respect—the notion that Black people were treated more violently and less fairly by the state, especially when the representation of the state was the police.

The city's mayor, G. T. Bynum, tried to gin up sympathy for the police, whose reputation was not aided by the report. "I feel for them [the Tulsa police officers], too, when I see them working this hard to be the best that they can be for the citizens of Tulsa, and then to have some attorney who is suing the city for millions of dollars get up and act like they are not doing anything. I don't think it is right." The attorney was a familiar person, a descendant of Cow Tom.

Although the city councillors voted unanimously to hold open meetings, they could not have predicted the level of stored-up anger and fear that poured from residents. It was, as veteran *Tulsa World* reporter Kevin Canfield put it, "unrelenting." People castigated the mayor, councillors, city police, and Tulsa as a whole for treating the city's Black residents worse than they do other residents.

But it shouldn't have surprised anyone in attendance that they and the city faced the tumult they did that day.

Tulsa has a spotty history on race, one made more complex by the Black Creeks, like the Perrymans, and Black Cherokees along with non-Indigenous Black people who witnessed Tulsa transform from a small lot of Native land to the Oil Capital of the World. Many of these same Black people watched the emergence of Black Wall Street in Tulsa as well as its decline. Black Wall Street—or as Booker T. Washington called it, Negro Wall Street—was a business and residential district that during the first decades of the twentieth century had one of the country's highest concentrations of Black success. It wasn't necessarily a bastion of extreme Black success, despite the soaring rhetoric often used in mythologizing Black Wall Street. Instead, it was a place of enormous opportunity, where being wildly successful, devastatingly destitute, and anything in between seemed to be equally likely. Within short walks, the area's residents could visit 191 businesses that populated the neighborhood, buy and sell products, and pay for services with relative assurance that the money would change hands twelve times before making its way outside the community. On the landscape of this bustling town were Black doctors, Black teachers, Black lawyers, Black children going to Black schools. Black hoteliers established the Stradford Hotel. Entertainment on Friday could be found at negro juke joints, and at theaters like the Dixie and the Dreamland. Yes, many in the neighborhood worked in predominantly white Tulsa. But the growing success of the city and the state had not missed Tulsa's Black community. Despite the fact that the Black people who lived in this neighborhood took different paths to getting to it—some through their Native American citizenship, some through their enslavement to Native Americans, some searching for a better life, and some escaping the increased violence in the post-Reconstruction South—they were all members of this organic experiment. And for a time, it seemed as if it was working.

Tulsa then, like now, was booming. A burgeoning oil capital, Tulsa was attracting new residents from other parts of the state and from states along the East Coast. For many, the city was quickly becoming the place to make it in America. And the growth of this city was apparent everywhere. "It was difficult to find even standing room on the trains," wrote a then-recent transplant, William Phillips, in his personal account of early times in Tulsa; he moved before the 1921 massacre and lived in Tulsa for the rest of his life. The city's population went from 18,000 in 1910 to 140,000 by 1930. And its oil and gas roots attracted all sorts of people to work in those industries—including, as William "Choc" Phillips, an aspiring vaudevillian, put it, "geologists, drillers, tool-dressers, pipeliners, teamsters, roustabouts, [and] roughnecks." And these workers needed grocery stores, barbershops, schools, and the like, and these shops filled out the frame of this city gushing with opportunity.

Tulsa's growth was also bursting in its Black neighborhoods. Though you could find some Black people living in different parts of the city, just north of the city's downtown quickly became known as Black Tulsa, Greenwood, Black or Negro Wall Street—a term given to several prosperous Black communities across America—and Little Africa. Even today, if you hear "North Tulsa," it's often synonymous with all these names.

If you've read or watched anything about Tulsa in the past few years, it's likely highlighted the accomplishments of wealthy men like O. W. Gurley, the putative founder of Black Wall Street; or J. B. Stradford, owner of the Stradford Hotel, which in the HBO show *Lovecraft Country* hosted Tic Freeman's family. But these stories gloss over the real wonder of this place—that any unknown Black person had the opportunity to forge their own success.

One such seemingly unknown person who might be a symbol of success—someone whose life didn't make it into the pages of my Oklahoma textbooks, along with most of the history of this part of town—was Rebecca Brown Crutcher. As a teenager in the 1920s, she owned and operated a barbecue pit near the railroad tracks that transported railmen to and from their work sites. Crutcher was a Black woman who lived in a Black neighborhood where Black success was feasible. Imagine a district that housed the majority of the city's Black residents who were not all rich and prosperous but who had real opportunity to prosper, even in 1921.

Residents could shop at hundreds of businesses, take out books at the library, and visit doctors' offices. Crutcher could shop at thirty-eight grocery stores, fruit stands, vegetable stands, and meat markets, according to Scott Ellsworth, the author of *The Ground Breaking: An American City and Its Search for Justice* and the canonical text on all things Black Wall Street, *Death in a Promised Land*. She could walk to and eat at more than two dozen restaurants, getting, as Ellsworth puts it, "everything from sandwiches and plate lunches to steaks and chops with all the trimmings."

But even as Tulsa was booming for Black families as well as their white counterparts, the city was growing more racist. If Tulsa's success had not skipped over Black Wall Street, neither did Tulsa's racial hate. In fact, it came to be targeted directly at Black Wall Street.

On May 30, 1921, an accident between a Black shoeshine boy named Dick Rowland and a white female elevator operator, Sarah Page, was intentionally misinterpreted as assault. To the white residents of Tulsa, this provided the pretext for what happened the

next day: white residents of Tulsa burned to the ground the thirty-
five square blocks and forty acres of this epicenter of Black
commerce. More than five thousand Black residents were arrested,
hundreds were killed, and even more were injured and admitted to
the city's hospitals. The fire engulfed nearly all that was Black Wall
Street. The next day, lights came on in white Tulsa, while in Black
Tulsa, those not detained in internment camps were trying to light
their way with the fires they built from the wood that came from the
wreckage of what was once their homes. Black Tulsans spent the
following winter using the charred remains of their flattened homes
to light flames to keep them warm.

The lingering image of this massacre and the conspiracy of si-
lence around it that the state was accused of years later fuel the interactions today between Black and white Tulsans in City Hall.
There, perfunctory discussions about food access are painted with a
racial lens, and the racial lens of Tulsa's Black citizens is tinted with
skepticism that politicians are in any way aligned with their interests. Dozens of Black Tulsans went before the city council in 2019
and told its members why, in James Baldwin's words, to be "a Negro
in this country and to be relatively conscious is to be in a state of
rage almost, almost all of the time . . . in the face of the most extraordinary and criminal indifference, indifference of most white
people in this country, and their ignorance."

To persuade the city councillors to approve public meetings on
these Equality Indicators, especially concerning law enforcement,
Tulsa resident and community activist Tiffany Crutcher told her
family's story. She traced a direct line of the devastating effects of racism in their long history of pain, from her great-grandmother's barbecue joint that once stood on Black Wall Street to her brother

Terence's death, unarmed, at the hands of white police officer Betty Shelby in 2016. Shelby was acquitted of first-degree manslaughter, and like many other police officers in America who shoot unarmed Black men, she got another job in the sheriff's office and has been asked to lecture other officers on how to deal with high-stress experiences. Is it any wonder that only about one in five black Tulsa residents trusts the city's police department?

Standing in front of her brother's personal effects that she'd strewn across the dais, Tiffany said: "Every day I look at this. My brother's bloody clothes, his shoes, his necklace, his socks, his prosthetic eye." She turned to the mayor of Tulsa, G. T. Bynum, and said, "Mayor Bynum, you said [at an earlier city council meeting] Thursday was simply a PR stunt. You think my brother being slaughtered by a killer cop is a PR stunt? Do you think my parents coming up here every single week is a PR stunt? . . . The fact that I would fly back and forth every single month to fight [for] police reform, you think that's a PR stunt? I was shocked when I heard you say that."

Why would Crutcher say this? Because the week before, Mayor Bynum had wondered about the value of these public meetings that discussed policing in the Black community. Mayor Bynum said, "Whether hearings are serious fact-finding sessions by city councilors or PR stunts by trial lawyers suing the city, we are going to stay focused doing the hard work of making Tulsa a place of equal opportunity for everyone."

Who were these lawyers Bynum was referring to? "I was not talking about the whole [community] event . . . I was talking about [Damario Solomon-Simmons's] comments at, before and during, the event," Bynum said. But the mayor was lobbing critiques at an attorney who he seemed to believe was bent on ruining the good name of Tulsa. To reporters after the meeting, Bynum asked, "Do I think their attorney jumps in front of the cameras every chance he gets to belittle the Tulsa Police Department and to belittle the hard work of so many people in our community who are trying to do work on community policing? Yeah, I do. To have some attorney who is suing the city for millions of dollars get up and act like [the police officers] are not doing anything, I don't think it is right," he said.

Damario, like his great-grandfather Jake Simmons Jr., doesn't care about offending the sensitivities of white men. Damario sued the City of Tulsa for what he found to be systemic racism toward Black people. His reaction and behavior were similar to those of his great-grandfather, who had financed a lawsuit against the City of Muskogee for denying Black people equal treatment under the law.

In a follow-up story in the *Tulsa World* was a copy of a letter Damario had written to the mayor. In the letter, Damario noted that Bynum had employed a winning election strategy of appealing to Black voters who felt completely shut out by the immediate past mayor, Dewey Bartlett. Damario remarked that "racial disparities in policing in Tulsa motivated [Bynum] to run for mayor." Damario had a point: when it was reported that Black Tulsans were arrested twice as often as any other race in Tulsa, Bynum had indignantly said, "This is precisely the type of issue that drove me to run for mayor . . . these are the issues I've called the great moral issue of our time in this city."

But to Damario, the actions of the mayor didn't match Damario's expectations. "Instead of engaging the hundreds of Tulsans who showed an unprecedented level of civil engagement related to ending anti-Black policing in Tulsa, Mayor Bynum focused his attention on personally attacking me for doing my job.

"Law is my ministry and justice is my passion," Damario wrote. So when the mayor dismissed him and his impending suit as a PR stunt, Damario struck back. He brought in the NAACP's Legal Defense Fund to launch investigations into the nature of policing in Tulsa.

This kind of civic activism—of portraying a truthful picture of Black life—runs in this family. From Cow Tom, who defied what expectations Ethan Allen Hitchcock placed on him and became a Creek chief, to Legus Perryman for being just "a nigger and a bad one at that" and ascending to principal chief, to Jake Sr. being considered among "the Negro-Creek [population who] has all of the natural born callousness of the genuine criminal," the Simmons family has a knack for repudiating the prevailing thoughts of white supremacy toward Black people. And that includes Damario Solomon-Simmons.

As articulate as Damario's written and verbal protests had become, less than twenty years earlier Damario would likely not have written this letter, in part because he had not yet become a Simmons. Without the intervention of fate, providence, or luck, Damario might never have *become* one at all.

DAMARIO SOLOMON TOOK the long way to the legal profession. He graduated last in his high school class, preferring football and weed over the rigorous academic expectations of his high school, Booker T. Washington, one of Oklahoma's best public schools. Instead of pursuing the academic dreams of his ancestors, he worked unloading boxes at a warehouse in Texas. He eventually ended up in Tahlequah, Oklahoma, taking classes at Northeastern State University—a school not known for its high academic standards—trying to get back on track, only to drop out.

"I was tripping over myself," Damario admitted. He was a pre-eminent football talent with an ax to grind. He eventually got to the University of Oklahoma in the 1990s, walked onto the football team, and played for one of the top programs in the country. People assumed that Damario had finally arrived. But he hadn't. His name was Damario Solomon and his journey to understanding himself was only beginning.

Damario's trips to the university library weren't to check out books. He found himself there more often than not trying to find himself, trying to discover a story that could explain why he felt a yearning to become more than who he was. But the answers to his questions would not be found in the library stacks. Instead they came through what Damario called "providence."

One day in the Bizzell Memorial Library on the campus of the University of Oklahoma, an elderly woman walked up to him and said, "Young man!" in the way only senior Black women can.

"Yes, ma'am?" Damario didn't know the woman, but he knew of her. She was Mrs. Rayella. And though to this day he can't recall her last name, he knew that Mrs. Rayella was the sort of elderly Black woman who was always addressed with a prefix and her first name. Damario had never met her, but whenever he was in the OU library, he noticed that she stared at him.

Her first words to him didn't make much sense to Damario: "You're a Simmons."

Damario's immediate but respectful reaction was: "Simmons? Ma'am, who are the Simmonses?"

Barreling on, Mrs. Rayella told Damario that his paternal grandmother, Johnnie Mae Austin, was born a Simmons to John Simmons, Jake Jr.'s brother.

Damario wasn't sure what to say. "I don't know my grandmother Johnnie Mae well," answered Damario, "but her last name is Austin."

But Mrs. Rayella was insistent. "Your grandmother's maiden name was Simmons."

The linebacker still didn't know what to say. When Damario was growing up, he saw his father only sporadically. Each weekend when his father visited, he would try to tell Damario about the "legends" in his background.

For Damario, the story he heard of Blacks being both fully Black and fully Creek was as strange then as it is to most people today. And his father's relative absence in his life created distance between Damario and his father's family, these legends he heard about. In addition, the strangeness of the Black Creeks' story made the retelling of his ancestors' histories confusing. So Damario handled his father's stories as most kids do: mentally he filed them away, never to return to them.

Yet he never really forgot these stories. His journey toward becoming a Simmons had begun.

Damario remembered how his father would talk about his ancestors Jake Simmons Sr. and Jake Simmons Jr. He remembered his father's tales and left that library with more questions than answers. His identity had been shaken as his curiosity had been piqued.

TO BE CLEAR, all Damario had learned was his grandmother's maiden name. But it wasn't until he sat in an African and African

American Studies class that he realized that his town and his neighborhood were on display as the professor discussed perhaps the state's most violent act of racism, the 1921 devastation of Black Wall Street.

A year after Mrs. Rayella's revelation, Damario stumbled across an important shortcut. It was in Tahlequah, Oklahoma, where he was giving a speech.

After his speech, a darker-skinned man than Damario, with slicked-back graying hair and large, auto-tinting prescription glasses approached him. The man's name was Don Simmons, and he said he was Damario's great-uncle. He said four words that would forever change Damario:

"You're one of mine."

Don took Damario to his house, where he detailed the histories of some of the "legends" that his father had spoken to him about. Don recalled what it was like to work with his father, Jake Simmons Jr., in the oil business, and he explained what it was like visiting his grandad's massive ranch outside Haskell. History—Damario's history—was becoming personal.

Don told Damario about Cow Tom, an ancestor of theirs who had advised generals during the Second Seminole War and who negotiated treaties with the U.S. government without any formal legal training. He told him of the land that contained the graves of people like Jake Simmons Sr. and Jr., who built wealth on the acreage that had been allocated to them as full Creek citizens.

Decades later, Damario still can recall that conversation. His identity within a single night was transformed, his family history suddenly richer and more complex than it had ever been. Story by story, Don equipped Damario with a new identity: a sense of self, filled with the histories of ancestral triumph.

The meeting with Don catalyzed Damario to take up the causes of those whose voices had been muted by the noise of a whitewashed history. The two became close, talking frequently as Damario continued to ask questions about his family. Don used each conversation as an opportunity to draw Damario into another level of insight into his identity.

During one of these conversations Don told Damario, "Who is a Solomon? Change your name to Simmons!"

Nearly two years after that first meeting, Don died, at age sixty-seven. Damario honored Don's last request to him by hyphenating his last name: Solomon-Simmons. As Damario put it, "I used to think I was a whole person, but when I met Don, I realized that I was missing half of who I was. Don was the gateway to becoming not just whole, but full."

In Oklahoma, being a Simmons meant that one cannot stand on the sidelines. Cow Tom wanted a grist mill for his family and a school that his children could attend. Jake Simmons Sr. wanted a ranch and a home to accommodate a large family. Jake Jr. wanted to be an oilman, and Johnnie Mae wanted to keep getting her mail from the Nation that her family helped lead.

But Cow Tom understood that the road to security for his children was to negotiate a deal with the U.S. government that secured Black freedom and then to convince senators that the same Black freedom inscribed in the Treaty of 1866 would stay secure. Jake Sr. might have wanted to live out his days on his ranch, but he also had to add his voice to the growing number of Black people in Oklahoma who had an inviolate claim to the land. Jake Jr. could've easily watched racism fester in his state, but instead he took his town to the Supreme Court. And Johnnie Mae might have wanted just to keep getting her mail, but her relentless connection to her identity inspired her grandson decades later to continue her work to be recognized as fully Creek.

Damario knew that because of who his ancestors had been and what they did to preserve, protect, and defend their identity, he had a duty to advocate for them and for himself.

IN THE TWENTY-FIRST CENTURY, Damario Solomon-Simmons is who you call in Oklahoma when racial injustice springs up. "Law is my ministry, but justice is my passion," he said. I would slightly revise this to say that while law is perhaps his ministry and justice may be his passion, it is becoming who he was meant to be that fuels his pursuit of justice.

To paraphrase Ralph Ellison, when we discover who we are, perhaps by understanding who we have been, we will be free. And freedom for those who have not been free is scary.

Damario understands this. As someone who is clear on what he is owed, he is ready to demand that he be paid.

The best way to know that someone is fighting for his identity is that he's consistently trying to understand himself. With Damario, it started first not with his own Creek citizenship but with that of someone else: Ron Graham.

IMAGINE YOUR IDENTITY being relegated to what happened to your family decades before you were born. Imagine your story being retold incorrectly—or not told at all.

This is the story of Ron Graham and another step in Damario's journey to becoming fully Black and fully Creek.

In 2005, *The Daily Oklahoman*, the student newspaper at the University of Oklahoma, published a piece that carried the headline "OU Lecturer Defends Citizenship of Creek Freedmen."

> An OU lecturer gave his closing argument Wednesday in what he called a very important case for people of black and American Indian heritage. Damario Solomon Simmons, an African-American studies lecturer at OU who is also a lawyer, is representing two black Creek men, Ron Graham and Fred Johnson, who want their citizenship reinstated in the Muscogee (Creek) Nation.

"To work with a case of this magnitude has been a very humbling experience," Solomon-Simmons told the reporter. "This case is of tremendous importance because it helps thousands of disenfranchised people find justice."

Physically Ron Graham and Damario Solomon-Simmons have a lot in common. They're both Black and bald, and they were born and brought up in Oklahoma. That is likely all that the registrar at the Creek Nation's citizenship office saw of the two when they tried repeatedly to get their citizenship papers.

But Ron and Damario are also very different. Ron knew nothing different from being fully Black and fully Creek. He didn't adopt Creek identity, he was born into it. "I was born and raised in the Creek Nation right there in Okmulgee," he said. His Blackness didn't preclude his Creek identity. In fact, his Blackness gave him a unique story to tell.

Ron Graham isn't a young man. His father, Theodore Graham, who went by "Blue," was listed on the Dawes Rolls as a Freedman on April 26, 1906. Growing up, Ron—like Johnnie Mae—would hear the Creek language floating through the house, as his father talked to him in the language of his own upbringing.

Blue Graham routinely made his way to Arkeba (often called "Abihka") Stomp Groups, where his father was featured prominently as a Pow-Wow star leader.

Ron's great-great-grandfather was listed on a document called the Loyal Creek Roll back in 1870. It was the list of Creek citizens who chose to side with the United States during the Civil War. For Graham, being Creek runs in the family because it is family.

Years had passed since 1979, the year of Ron's father's death and the death of Black life in the Creek Nation. The expulsion of Black people from the Nation had gone unnoticed by Ron, just as it had gone unnoticed for Johnnie Mae until she realized she had stopped getting Creek mail. But Blue's death triggered Ron to attempt to start researching his Creek heritage. Like many of us, he knew who he was but he wanted to find the remnants of who had come before him to build a firmer foundation for his identity. That foundation would include becoming what Ron called a "card-carrying citizen of the Creek Nation."

Blue Graham would have carried a card that nearly every Creek knows well: CDIB—the Certificate of Degree of Indian Blood. Many who are citizens of the Creek Nation have a small laminated card with a unique identifying number called an EDN, their address, and at times a percentage breakdown of just how "Creek" they are—which is an unscientific blood quantum. This CDIB card would become for Ron an elusive piece of the puzzle of his identity.

After his father's death, Ron started to ask how to get a CDIB card. The answer became clear very quickly: "Go to Okmulgee, not

Muskogee, Oklahoma, and apply for citizenship within the Muscogee (Creek) Nation."

In 1983, Ron went to the Creek Nation's headquarters in Okmulgee. He saw it as an opportunity to reestablish a connection with his
father, to become more involved in the history of his ancestors, and
to recall the days when his parents and generations before them
claimed their loyalty to the Creek Nation.

On the corner of North Wood, U.S. 75, and Highway 56 stood
the complex of Creek government buildings, the physical remnants
of what should be an autonomous, self-governing Nation. Ron Graham walked in only to be directed to the Bureau of Indian Affairs
office five minutes' drive away. The representatives at the Creek Nation told him he'd have to apply for citizenship there. So he went to
the very symbol of colonialism to inquire what he must do to become officially Creek.

The BIA official told Ron that if he wanted to enroll in the Nation, he would have to have a direct lineal ancestor enrolled as Creek
on the Dawes Rolls. What would have initially thrown off most people found Ron giving the official the name of his father, Theodore
"Blue" Graham, who, Ron knew, was listed on the 1906 Dawes Rolls.

The BIA officer went back through the files and returned to tell
Ron that Blue Graham wasn't on the Dawes Rolls. Blue and Ron,
according to the official, were descended from a Creek Freedman.

Ron, confused, told the officer he had no idea what it meant to be
a Creek Freedman. His father had always whistled Creek songs,
spoke Creek at home, and attended Creek Pow-Wows as a star leader.

Ron insisted that his father was Creek Indian.

The BIA officer flattened Ron's history with a deafening blow of
oversimplification.

"Creek Freedmen were not really Creek," Ron recalled the officer telling him. They were just the "former slaves of the Creek Nation." To make matters worse, Ron was told Black Freedmen "did not possess any 'real Indian blood.'"

Damario recalled that his client Ron left the BIA "dejected" and "humiliated." But this was all too similar to the stories of his own grandmother—those in which she was denied the continuation of her own citizenship in a Nation that was once led by her family.

By 1984, Ron had started researching his family history in earnest, collecting documents and photographs. He located his father's Creek enrollment card, which had all of his children and his wife listed on it. With these documents, Ron returned to the BIA in Okmulgee, this time with confidence that the documents would validate that he was Creek.

But the BIA told Ron what he had been told the first time: *Your family is listed on the Freedmen Roll, and as such your father has no Creek blood, no matter what he or his family thought.*

Two years later, Ron tried again. He made his way back to the BIA, and this time a different official told him that for him to qualify for membership, his ancestors had to have a blood degree—in other words, they had to have ancestors listed on the "by blood" roll and not the Freedmen Roll. This helped Ron, as it was specific advice. Back to the research he went.

This time Ron learned that his first cousin on his father's side, Elmer Payne, was enrolled in the Creek Nation and got his CDIB card issued by the BIA—the same that had denied Ron his card and told him that he had no Creek blood. According to this card, Elmer was one-eighth Creek. Elmer's mother was Sissy Graham, Blue Graham's sister.

Ron put more miles on his car and made his way back to the Ok-mulgee BIA to ask how no Creek blood ran in him and his father if his first cousin Elmer and his aunt Sissy could be fully enrolled Creeks.

Instead of answering his question, the BIA official placed the burden of proving who Ron and his family were back on Ron. Rather than reckon with the racism that fueled this division, the official doubled down, telling Ron he had to find proof of an official "blood quantum of Muscogee (Creek) Indian blood" in his father.

Imagine having to find blood that doesn't exist—not because your father isn't Creek, but because blood quantum was an arbitrary maneuver engineered by white men to determine how little land Indigenous people could keep. The goal was to disempower these people and their society. There is no way to verify the Creek blood that people claim to have. People who have it have it only because a white man thought them Creek enough to be Creek and not too Black to dilute those who are Creek. Find the blood, they said, knowing that the blood isn't to be found.

This moment showed Ron that blood quantum wasn't science, it was thinly veiled racism that propped up a colonialist way of separating people to promote the economic and social interests of white America. He just found out the hard way.

Racist and wrong as these rules of blood quantum were, Ron Graham still wanted to be admitted to the Creek Nation. So over the next several years he learned to become an amateur archivist and a genealogist. To this day, librarians and researchers at the Oklahoma Historical Society direct anyone interested in learning about the Black Creeks to Ron Graham.

By 1993, Ron believed that he could show his father's family's blood quantum. He had uncovered a document that showed that Joe Hutton, his father's grandfather, was listed as having at least one-fourth Creek blood. Next, Ron's grandmother, a daughter of Joe Hutton, had a document called a Proof of Death and Heirship from the superintendent for the Five Civilized Tribes that indicated Joe Hutton was one-eighth Creek.

Armed with this documentation, Ron wrote directly to Jimmy Gibson, the superintendent of the Okmulgee BIA office, and demanded a meeting.

The meeting came a year later, on July 17, 1994. This time, Superintendent Gibson promised to look into what could be done, as the documents proved once and for all that Ron Graham was who he had always known himself to be: Creek. The next year Ron got a glimmer of hope when he received confirmation that his application was being processed. But later that year, he received another letter, rejecting his application. The reason? "Eligibility for an applicant to enroll in Muscogee (Creek) Nation Tribe must have an ancestor on the final roll of 1906," the letter read.

So Ron began again. The next year, he was back at the BIA's Okmulgee office. By this point, the BIA was no longer issuing enrollment cards. He would have to go to the Creek Nation's citizenship office. Perhaps he'd have a better chance there. But his Blackness and the Blackness of his ancestors still were too much for the Creek Nation to accept. Despite his documentation, he was told once again that as a Freedmen descendant, he wouldn't be eligible for Creek citizenship.

No one at the Bureau of Indian Affairs helped him. As with Damario, the injustice Ron faced was fuel for a new career. He became a professional genealogist specializing in the lives and ancestry of those who are Black and Indigenous. It took this vocational switch for him to realize not only that the enrollment process of the Dawes Commission was flawed and racist, but also that it never actually embodied scientific methods.

At the end of 1998, Ron went back to the Creek Nation armed with the skills and training of a professional genealogist. But that didn't matter to Creek officials—or so it seemed. He again filed for citizenship and received no response. He tried again in 2001, only for his application to be flat-out rejected. He tried again a year later, this time not just with the proof that his father had Creek citizenship, but with even more validation: thanks to his genealogical training, Ron learned that his father was on Dawes Roll Number 671 as a Creek Freedman. It included his paternal grandmother, Creasy Graham, whose Proof of Death and Heirship documents had been accepted by the Office of the Superintendent for the Five Civilized Tribes, which confirmed in detail that his father, Blue, was one-eighth Creek.

Despite this new information, Ron was told once again that as his father "was on the Freedman Roll," his application was denied. Once again, Ron Graham was too Black to be Creek, even if his ancestors had been.

IN 2004, Damario was a recent graduate of the University of Oklahoma College of Law and had returned to Tulsa. While many of his law school classmates went to work for large firms in Oklahoma City, Tulsa, Dallas, and Houston, Damario felt there were battles to wage that no large firm would ever embrace. So as his father and grandfather had done, Damario struck out on his own—back in Oklahoma. Though his first office was housed inside the offices of the Urban League of Tulsa in North Tulsa, Damario hung his shingle in the offices at the Petroleum Club Building at 601 South Boulder Avenue in downtown Tulsa. His full-time secretary, Vashti Butler, would manage the office, while his mother would help out from time to time.

Ron had heard of Damario Solomon-Simmons, a young Black lawyer who had become obsessed with *becoming*, so he approached him to represent him. Perhaps what made Damario so committed to Ron Graham and his cause wasn't just that Damario was Creek too. He also knew what it was like living with a limited version of your identity.

All of a sudden, he took on a cause most people hadn't considered: advocating for those on the margins of the margins to help them claim their rightful identities. For Damario, it was personal: Ron's story is his story. So Damario needed no convincing to take on the case. And it might seem odd: a Black man taking on a Nation that had been as beleaguered by the threats of white supremacy as any other for perpetuating the tenets of white supremacy that ultimately excluded him.

AMERICA'S JUDICIAL SYSTEMS have been the instruments that can sound the call for change or maintain the status quo. Within sixty years, the U.S. Supreme Court went from staunchly supporting the notion of separate but theoretical equality between races in *Plessy v. Ferguson* to dismantling that precedent in *Brown v. Board of Education*. Sometimes the courts give us hope that they might side with progress when we desperately need them to.

In the case of the Black Seminoles, the courts gave Black citizens of the Creek Nation hope and potentially a pathway toward achieving what they thought would be justice. In 2002, less than four years before *Ron Graham v. Muscogee (Creek) Nation of Oklahoma Citizenship Board*, Black Seminoles found themselves in a similar situation: excluded from membership in the Seminole Nation that had once accepted them. The Seminole Nation derived much of its cultural heritage and practices from the Creek Nation. Like the Creeks, they were "helped" by the Dawes Commission in the late nineteenth and early twentieth centuries and their lands reduced to a fraction of what they once were, taken over by a U.S. government greedy for land, a new Oklahoma state government hungry to make its mark and refine the contours of its boundaries, and private-sector actors who saw land and would soon see oil on that land. Like Black Creeks, Black Seminoles made up a distinguishable and substantial portion of the population living on Seminole lands. In fact, in 1900, nearly a third of all Seminoles in Indian Territory were Black. And like the Creek, the Seminole Nation signed a treaty with the U.S. government that guaranteed equal citizenship for both Blacks and Black Seminoles.

There were differences, however. When they reorganized their territory and government structure in 1969, the Seminoles relegated two townships to their Black citizens. Two representatives from the "Freedmen Towns" sat on the Seminole Nation's council. In a similar stroke of racism that was cloaked in Indigenous self-determination, the Seminole Nation of Oklahoma restricted its membership in 2000 to the blood quantum that the Seminoles rebuffed nearly one hundred years prior—just as the Creeks had done. As a result, many Black Seminoles faced the real threat of not continuing to be what they had been for generations: both Black and Seminole.

The Black Seminoles filed suit as Ron Graham did, but they had a different outcome because the leaders of the Department of the Interior were different from those when Ron applied. The Black Seminoles got a favorable ruling from the Department of the Interior: the department told the Seminole Nation that its status as a federally recognized Nation would be at stake if it did not allow Blacks who had been in the Nation all that time to participate in the franchise and to sit on the National Council as they once had.

In 2005, Ron and Damario filed a new suit against the Creek Nation in Creek courts. They believed the outcome would be similar to what had happened in the Black Seminole case and that the Creek Nation should be held to the Treaty of 1866 just as the Seminoles had been. They thought that their chance to begin again had come, that their long journey of becoming had finally seen its destination ahead.

Ron filed the suit in the Creek Nation District Court with the legal counsel of Damario. To do this, Ron had to exhaust all administrative appeals—which he had—so the failing to get citizenship over all those years had some legal merit. Oral arguments were heard in August 2005 and lasted several days. On March 17, 2006, the court issued a finding that read: "By not considering and failing to apply the laws of the Muscogee Creek Nation that [were] in effect when the Plaintiff's Application for Enrollment [was] initially presented, the Muscogee (Creek) Nation Citizenship Board acted contrary to the law and in an arbitrary and capricious manner."

Put simply, the court found that the citizenship board misapplied the law in denying Ron's claim of inclusion. Ron should have applied under a preexisting code of the Creek Nation called NCA 81-06, which was in effect long before the code that the citizenship board used to deny him citizenship. NCA 81-06 would entitle Ron to file for the citizenship he hoped for under the "by blood" distinction, though he would never be able to prove that he is a Creek by blood, because his father was listed as Freedman on the Dawes Rolls.

While this was not a victory, there was at least a glimmer of what might be considered hope. That is, until the Supreme Court of the Creek Nation weighed in. It took up the case and found that there was "no evidence that the Citizenship Board acted arbitrarily and capriciously," and overturned the state court's ruling.

As a result, Ron Graham became for many Black Creeks the paragon of fighting the good fight even when the fight seems fixed. Damario got his first brush with challenging a Nation that he also wanted to reclaim citizenship in that didn't want him back.

The reality was that long before Damario tried this case, the Creek Freedmen Band—a collection of Black people who could trace their identity back to ancestors who were once citizens of the Creek Nation—had a drumbeat going. This Freedmen Band started to collect stories from Black Creeks who could recall what it was like to be a citizen. They reached out far and wide. They held conference after conference, meeting after meeting. Flew in speakers. Spoke with members of Congress. Hosted educational seminars. Like Ron, they delved into the genealogical research by virtue of wanting to prove who they know themselves to be. Perhaps most important, Damario became their attorney, their go-to legal counsel on every suit they'd file going forward. Because while they might have known Damario Solomon, they came to rely on Damario Solomon-Simmons.

CHAPTER 14.

RADICAL MEMORIES

You like to think memory goes far back though
remembering was never recommended. Forget all
that, the world says. The world's had a lot of practice.
No one should adhere to the facts that contribute
to narrative, the facts that create lives.

CLAUDIA RANKINE, *CITIZEN:
AN AMERICAN LYRIC*

In some important sense, Damario's quest for justice has gone
unfulfilled. Since the Ron Graham case, he's taken the Creek
Nation to court, both in their courts and in the U.S. District
Court system. And each time he's entered those courts, he's left
without a win, and in the case of the District Court—unlike the
Cherokee Nation, which lost to its former Black citizens in 2017—he
only earned a dismissal. His argument is clear: You—"you" being
the Creek Nation—have to follow the law. He and his clients are
trying to claw back their claim to ancestry and identity using the

law. They refuse to forget, no matter how easy it is to do so. No matter how simple life could be if they accepted their Blackness without its former residence in the Nation that once accepted them, they are fighting for an identity, a complete identity. And they're asking all of us to do what often seems too radical for America: remember.

Remembrance is pain. Even remembering the good can induce pain. Remembering the good times when the good times have turned bad triggers the wincing we'd rather avoid. In America, we often choose to forget in order to avoid the pain. We assemble our individual and collective pasts based on where we want the status quo to stay now and in the future. As a society, we—inconveniently for those on the margins—construct our present and future on a history that absolves us from the pain.

Perhaps that's why we don't like to remember. Maybe that's why Damario is the aggravating nag to the Creek Nation, because even though circumstances for the Creek could always be better, considering that they too live on the margins of society, his existence, his constant reminders of who his family has been, indict everything about the exclusive life the Creeks lead and in turn the context within which our society has allowed this exclusion to take place. It reminds the Creek leadership that its present and future will remain incomplete without accepting the stories of Damario and his ancestors.

These incomplete present and future identities, however, are not limited to the case of Damario and his family, his clients, and their families. There was the project of turning the Creek Nation into a race that could set aside citizens like Johnnie Mae from other citizens. Thanks to the efforts of Dawes, this project created a litmus test that limited the extent to which one could construct its history upon the pain they had endured. And when Claude Cox, the chief of the Creek Nation, exclaimed that the "Negro would soon outnumber the Indian" and led the march to a new constitution that did not include the very "Negro" who counted the Creek Nation home, it too introduced a stumbling block for countless others to memorialize the lives of their families who had done so much to make the Creek Nation home. Claude Cox did the same thing that Henry Dawes had done. He declared who would and who would not be Creek without first considering the full measure of history that produced the moment in which he lived—though arguably Cox had more claim to do so than the white man from Massachusetts who wanted to "help." Chief Cox, however, did something far more dangerous. He discriminated against the Black citizens of his Nation and cloaked it as protection for an identity. But the identity Cox sought to protect had holes in its construction: it was ahistorical— dismissive, even.

By discounting the claim that Cow Tom's descendants have in the Creek Nation, Cox tried to invalidate their claim on history. And by invalidating their claim, he can claim the ultimate prize of white supremacy: getting those on the margins to adopt the very segregatory habits and practices they once bucked against.

We have seen this trajectory elsewhere. And it also reminds us that this constant upward trajectory—that life improves for those who wait long enough—is wrong.

But what do we become when we do not remember? Who are we if we avoid the past out of a fear of the pain?

Cow Tom and his descendants, as well as everyone who's taken up his cause over the years, have asked a fundamental question: How can we be truly moral people if we ignore who we are and where we came from? The answer, in short, is that we can't. Cow Tom, for

Ethan Allen Hitchcock, was Yargee's Negro, his Negro Tom. He was Black, and Creek, and was to Hitchcock undignified—nothing more than a Negro who belonged to another man. He, and all of us, can be and are, in fact, many things at once. Or in other words, we contain multitudes. Some call this intersectionality, the collision of identities. But others have put it more simply: "I am a narrative, someone's almost forgotten story. Remembered." You and I, Damario and Johnnie Mae. We are all narratives, aspects of which have been forgotten—often on purpose. But we don't fully become who it is that we want to be without first remembering who we have been.

You might be reading this fully initiated into the varied histories that brought you to this moment. You might (unlike me when I started writing this book) have the fullest and most comprehensive understanding of what it means to be you because you understand where you came from and who you are.

But in America, unless you're a white, binary, cisgender man—in other words, a straight white guy with some money or land whose identity and rights have never been on a referendum or on a court docket—your existence is protest and your decision to remember is radical.

JAMES BALDWIN ONCE REMARKED that to be African American is to be African without any memory and American without any privilege. While this is an apt description of what it means to be Black in America, it also could describe what it means to Black Creek. To be both Black and Creek is to be in a constant state of trying to persuade your country's history to give a damn about you. Because the history of those who tell it hasn't cared much about what it means to be Black or Creek. Damario Solomon-Simmons, Johnnie Mae Austin, and countless others have been striving to be remembered and included for who they are by telling us who their ancestors were. Contrary to Baldwin's observation, these Black Creeks had privilege once, but not necessarily in what we'd consider America. They got it by their heritage. But that heritage is fading. So they have made their lives about Sankofa.

"Go back and get it."

That is the charge implicit in the term "Sankofa." From the Twi language of Ghana, the term means the rescuing of what is being left behind. That is the idea the Black Creeks want to maintain. They know that there is a risk of Black Creek history being left behind and subsequently their identity. They know that if they don't start their Freedman Bands, host conferences, continue their archival work, file for their own tribal recognition, and file suits for reinclusion in the Creek Nation, their stories might be doomed to fade.

At the heart of Sankofa is the idea that memory of the past is the key to liberation in the future. We are not as simple as white supremacy tells us we are. We can learn that it is in celebrating our complexities that we begin to live abundantly. Remembering the various histories that brought us here is the first step to living empowered lives.

Damario's identity, for example, isn't simple; nothing about being both Black and Creek is. But his stories and those of his family make clear what is so abstract. Their claim to the American Dream came through the Creek Nation, a nation they helped to build. They've lost their citizenship, and this loss has changed their destiny. Their ancestors created the future that they wanted in a Nation that once enslaved Blacks. Damario is on a mission to reclaim that future.

Remembering's radical characteristics are best understood when we realize that we need our present and future to rectify the ugliness of our past. Often we remember to reconcile instead of remembering to repair. In my hometown of Tulsa, the Massacre of Black Wall Street has been remembered. City officials have issued halfhearted apologies about what happened many years ago—reflecting that elements of what happened were "harmful." They've built ornate memorials, a history center, and even a park called Reconciliation Park. But they have not fixed much of anything. What's wrong isn't just that Cow Tom's descendants aren't citizens of the Creek Nation. What's wrong is that our history books never told us about this. What's wrong is that we've lived our lives untethered to the history that could propel us toward justice. By virtue of knowing this story, you become a steward in this effort to "Go back and get it!" You now share in the responsibility of trying to appreciate fully the identities of people. You now have what it takes to understand that society's collective identity can bear the pain of remembering what portions of it have been left behind by white supremacy. You can now identify that those on the margins need allies who don't rush to reconciliation without accommodating for and rectifying the weightiness of the truth, which demands reconciliation, restitution, and reparation for those who have been aggrieved.

Claudia Rankine said it best: In America, "remembering was never recommended." We, on the margins, were supposed to take the lumps society gave us. And after taking our lumps, we were supposed to pretend that the lumps were never there. "Forget all that, the world says," Rankine reminds us. She tells us that "the world's had a lot of practice." It's why we expect Black folks and Brown folks to forget that redlining, mass incarceration, slavery, and inequitably funded education (to mention a few) have barred Black and Brown folks from opportunities that we deserve.

Perhaps we all bear the responsibility of expanding our moral imaginations by reconstructing our society's collective identity as one that embraces beautiful complex histories and cherishes the opportunities to tell those who have not mattered for so long that they do matter. We need to go back and get it so that we might become who we ought to be.

CHAPTER 15

REPARATIONS AND
THE BLACK CREEK

But black history does not flatter
American democracy; it chastens it.

Ta-Nehisi Coates

In 2003, I was sitting in my small, Christian, mostly white school
in Tulsa (I was one of two Black people to graduate in my class)
when I first heard of reparations. The school, St. Augustine Academy, 131 students in total from kindergarten through twelfth grade,
stood on Creek land, less than four miles from the cemetery where
Legus Perryman and other Black Creek leaders are buried. Despite
that proximity, my teachers, from elementary through high school,
all but one of whom were white, prided themselves on telling the
untold portions of history—often the parts they claimed the elite,
anti-Christian, liberal educational and media systems wouldn't tell:

that America was somehow a Christian nation. That usually meant telling stories about the untold history of leaders of Western thought. My high school history teacher, a white Calvinist whose credentials were in church history, mocked these "reparations" as a ludicrous excess, as a "step too far." And as a thirteen-year-old Black kid, I somehow agreed.

Reparations, I was taught, couldn't possibly be for me or my kind. I was lulled into thinking that reparations weren't necessary. Affirmative action was seen as the closest thing to reparations, and even that—prioritizing outreach and admission for people of color and women in getting jobs and into schools—was beyond reasonable consideration. But come Black History Month, we were allowed to remember a few legislative bills (with the titles "Civil Rights" or "Voting Rights" or "Fair Housing"), actions of the Black people my white teachers liked, and a holiday named after Dr. King (which for years I didn't get off because my school didn't consider it a legitimate holiday). What we were encouraged to forget was everything else: the centuries of violence and inequality against Black people, the centuries of white supremacy, and the centuries of struggles of people like the Black Creek, who didn't fit neatly into the American myth.

From where I sat, at age thirteen in an Oklahoma classroom, the rise of Black opportunity in America need not be cheapened through tangible benefits. Instead, the lofty language about equity and equality was enough. And perhaps even more precisely, targeting efforts to remember and repair the historical damages visited upon any particular race or ethnic group seemed patently unfair. Regrettably, many people still think like I did at thirteen years old.

But don't feel bad: plenty of self-proclaimed political leaders don't think much differently from how I did back then. In 2019, the U.S. House of Representatives took up a bill to investigate reparations, House Resolution 40. When asked what he thought of the bill, the Senate majority leader, Mitch McConnell of Kentucky, said, "I don't think reparations for something that happened 150 years ago for whom none of us currently living are responsible is a good idea." Arguing that the country should not even study reparations, McConnell added, "We've tried to deal with our original sin of slavery by fighting a civil war, by passing landmark civil rights legislation. We elected an African American president."

This assessment of our past doesn't just miss the mark; it willfully obscures how deliberately a white supremacist government has systematically undermined and destroyed generations of Black lives. Our culture has become captivated by the question of whether reparations are a worthy goal. Yet as we debate this question, we do so grounded in seemingly elusive, abstract concepts—the "original sin of slavery," for example—while avoiding the countless examples of Black suffering rooted in concrete experiences. And those concrete experiences lie around us. But in the case of the Black Creeks, their experiences lie beyond the extent of our moral imagination, stifled by an intentionally limited understanding of history.

On the day of the H.R. 40 hearing, Ta-Nehisi Coates testified before the committee, saying, "Many of us would love to be taxed for the things we are solely and individually responsible for. But we are American citizens, and thus bound to a collective enterprise that extends beyond our individual and personal reach." The challenge for all those who seek to bring our past to life is how to connect today's readers with a seemingly distant collective enterprise.

Perhaps the story of the Black Creeks is that tool. Hearing the stories of Johnnie Mae no longer getting mail from the Creek Nation. Of Ron Graham trying so hard to preserve his ancestors' history. Of the relief the Cherokee Freedmen and their descendants like Kenneth Cooper and Marilyn Vann felt when they gained citizenship in the Nation their ancestors had helped to build. These stories show the real-world consequences of the United States' willingness to let history fade from forming our identities. These stories represent an unadulterated retelling of our history, no matter how ugly. Exploring this story has been an open invitation to rescue a critical issue from being overlooked. The stories of Cow Tom and his descendants provide the historical and contemporary blueprints to understand reparations.

Carla Pratt, a legal scholar and dean of Washburn University School of Law, once wrote, "To me, the term 'reparations' is much broader than [monetary payment or merely financial compensation for slave labor]." She, like the Black Creeks who want to reclaim their citizenship, subscribes to a broader, more nuanced view of reparations. For them, it is not a static, transactional experience but a movement to reclaim American history. For Pratt, "this form of reparations requires thorough investigation into what actually happened and prods us to ask how and why it happened."

This is what the Simmons family has been doing. Their lawsuits have established fact bases that show how their citizenship has been stripped—Damario and his clients would argue unjustly—and they have prodded the Creek Nation and the U.S. Department of the Interior to answer why it happened. Though we know the answer: being Black in America has become, in the eyes of many, destructive to any other identity they might hold.

What this requires is for us to, as Pratt writes, "stop retelling the story from the perspective of the people who have traditionally had the voice and tell new stories from the perspective of those who have been subordinated and silenced." Damario's family have had their stories told by those who cast aside their memories of their ancestors as too Black to be fully Creek. What they want from their lawsuits is, as Carla Pratt has written, to "restore their humanity [and to] reclaim a lost perspective for the nation's history."

That's the power of their stories, restoring a perspective on America's history that could be all but lost.

THESE STORIES also have changed me. That thirteen-year-old version of myself thought of reparations as "too far," "too radical," and "too difficult."

At that time, the notion of reparations was fundamentally at odds with what I believed about Black progress. Reparations were tactile and tangible—a repayment for how the country subdued and subjugated Blackness over centuries—while my notions of Black progress were stuck in the theoretical: for example, the idea of setbacks to equality being only temporary, since the universe bent toward justice. I allowed theoretical questions to complicate every imagined challenge to implementing reparations: "How could we pay for this?" "Should I, a son of Jamaican immigrants, benefit from reparations?" "Would white people ever go for tax dollars from every paycheck going toward paying for sins they don't think they personally committed?"

These questions caused me to doubt the legitimacy of reparations. I needed new stories to understand how linear and direct and calculable the damage done to Black life in America had been. I needed those stories to understand what was owed and how the fact that what was owed was not being paid has impacted our sense of justice in America. Or perhaps I needed to see ancient stories—like those of the Black Creek—in new ways. The stories of people who realize that America comes up short in what is owed to Black people. Even Black people like me.

It wasn't until I traced the transfer of injustice down generations that I understood the moral imperative of reparations. Because the stories of Cow Tom and his descendants showed me that there has always been another way to be Black than what America has told us.

CHAPTER 16

AMERICAN COLLATERAL

In ways so embedded that it is rarely apparent, the set of
assumptions, privileges, and benefits that accompany the status
of being white have become a valuable asset that whites sought
to protect and that those who passed sought to attain. . . .

Only white possession and occupation of land was validated
and therefore privileged as a basis for property rights.

CHERYL HARRIS

I've often bristled at the notion that America has always been
a great country. In many important senses, America is a great
country, but it's particularly great at building a narrative of continued forward progress. Today was better than yesterday. Yesterday was better than the day before. And tomorrow will be better
than all the days before it. We bet on our future because we believe
our future is secured, but our country bets on its success with extreme confidence, in part because we have been great at accepting a

certain amount of collateral damage—and Black and Native life in America has often been that acceptable collateral. But in the case of this family—the Simmons family—Black Native life has been the ideal form of collateral. Tomorrow was always going to be better for large segments of our country because time and time again we collateralized Black life.

Black life, Native life, and Black Native life in America have been endlessly used as collateral, as the cost of building a nation that takes little of these lives into account. To build the wealth of this country, Black bodies had been used without consent and without compensation. And centuries later, when these descendants ask for their piece of the pie—for reparations—they have been told it is unfair to receive a piece of what they built.

To found and to grow this country, Native land was co-opted, Native customs sacrificed to make way for a life that white people— colonizers, government leaders, farmers, businessmen—thought would be better for themselves.

We saw it when we learned that Cow Tom was called "his Negro Tom" by Ethan Allen Hitchcock. In Hitchcock's eyes, his worthiness was tied to the servitude he offered the chief, Yargee. When Benjamin Hawkins collateralized Indigenous life and its varied customs in order to boost the economic prosperity of America, he attempted to diminish, intentionally or unintentionally, Native American life. When his acolytes sought to deal with the "Indian Problem" and when his predecessors and successors tried to deal with the "Negro Problem," they all tried to minimize them to the parts of their identity that were useful for the advancement of an American identity that didn't include them. Black people's and Native people's identities were relegated to items on rolls—their holdings on lands diminished and their stake in the promise of the American Dream limited by whatever concessions America thought it least discomforting to its white citizens to give them.

Senators Dawes and Bixby reduced what had been set aside as Native land and Black Native land, guaranteeing that white settlers would co-opt land and opportunities that had belonged to their Native and Black counterparts. Then Dawes and Bixby went further by creating identity parameters and racializing Creek identity. They made claims race-based: if you were Black or Black Creek, you became less valuable, less worth fighting for, and someone whose rights became worth trampling over to achieve the vision of America that was just that much less accommodating.

And Chief Claude Cox, Estelusti himself—the remnants of Black identity running through his veins—used the rich beauty of Creek and Black Creek identity to make the Creek Nation even more independent from the dictates of the U.S. government.

We have done this in America for hundreds of years. We accept minimizing nonwhite life in America to help us maintain the status quo. The idea of Black lives being pushed further to the margins had become so entrenched in our national character that expelling Black Creeks from the Creek Nation became a worthwhile way to carve a path of independence for the Creek Nation—a path charted and led by a white government.

Perhaps by reincluding the Black Creek—the very people whose ancestors led the Creek Nation—in the Creek Nation is how we begin this critical project of valuing the very people who became collateral damage in the messy business of the United States.

If the stories of Cow Tom, the Black Creeks, and their long strug-gle teach us anything, it is that our humanity should not be thrown aside to achieve anything. In creating what's best for tomorrow, America should rely on the collective strength of our humanity, not the value that one part of our society can extract from it.

CHAPTER 17

EMPOWERMENT, NOT DILUTION

History, with its hard spine & dog-eared
Corners, will be replaced with nuance

TRACY SMITH, "SCI-FI"

B orn in New York City and raised there for the first eight years
of my life, I attended a church full of Jamaican, Trinidadian,
and Bahamian immigrants, pastored by my Jamaican grandfather. In my home, I had two Jamaican parents. And my church
friends—the only friends I was allowed to have in my strict, slightly
Pentecostal household—were all the sons and daughters of those same
Caribbean immigrants. Thanksgiving dinners, church potlucks, and
Easter dinners—which we'd call Resurrection Sunday because somehow Easter was pagan—came replete with all the quasi–soul food
American fixings laid messily next to Caribbean staples.

When we moved to Oklahoma, I attended predominantly white schools, where I was asked indelicate questions about my race. In reply, I'd stumble over a complex set of half-truths: "Well . . . I'm Black, but I'm Jamaican, but not directly from Jamaica, from New York, but my parents are Jamaican, but they immigrated decades ago and don't sound that Jamaican unless they're upset at me for not doing the dishes." Eventually, I'd just masquerade and align myself with the larger diaspora, simply answering, "I'm Black."

But nearly every Black Creek I've met tells me something both authentic and radical: "I'm both fully Black and fully Creek." They contained multitudes and each time they told me, their proclamation compelled me to recognize the multitudes I contain. To not be fully both diminishes an important part of our history that some of our country want to forget. Simplifying the identity of a person to fit in a category is a degradation of critical history and, even more, their claim on who they have been, who they are, and who they can become. If this history were appreciated, it could have a major impact on the Black Creek because it would also be true to how they view themselves.

Imagine if Cow Tom's descendants are right: perhaps Cow Tom being recorded as a slave was just the simplification of identity run amok. Maybe Ethan Allen Hitchcock, the young colonel who chronicled Cow Tom's life, just couldn't wrap his mind around the notion that a Black man could be simultaneously free, never enslaved, and fully Creek. And perhaps today we are similarly too wedded to our notions of who people are or who people are not. We let our simplistic misconceptions about race triumph rather than allow identities to be beautifully complex.

For decades, members of the Creek Nation and many other Native Americans worried about the purity of their blood, a concern they didn't have until white settlers who coveted their land told them they should care about this distinction. This is why they began anchoring their citizenship "by blood." They made their Nations, which are legally political entities, into race-simplifying institutions—Nations that destroy the opportunity for Black Creeks to be fully Black and fully Creek. To the Creek Nation, these Black Creeks, despite their well-documented claims to being Creek, are imperfections that dilute true "Creekness." Cow Tom's descendants, Legus Perryman's descendants, and countless other Black Creeks have rebuffed this for decades, confidently claiming that they are both fully Black and fully Creek. But being fully Black and fully Creek and embracing all that comes from both identities can be dangerous to our more simplistic patriotism. It tells America that Blackness and Indigeneity are not dilutive on their own or together. Instead, they are empowering. But empowering Black lives represents the undoing of white supremacy. White supremacy even when it is conveyed as "help" has as its main goals the words of Henry Dawes: "The work is accomplished when the Indian has become one of us." And the only way this goal could be accomplished is if people like Dawes—like Hawkins before him, and Washington before him—could wash away the memories that made them. The goal of white supremacy is to frame identities and their value in relation to whiteness: the closer to white, the better. Put another way: if Cow Tom, Jake Simmons Sr., his son Jake Simmons Jr., Jake Jr.'s grandniece Johnnie Mae, and her grandson Damario Solomon take control of the narratives of their own identity history and actively fight to reclaim what's theirs, this disconnects them from needing to define themselves separate from the white perspective that Washington, Hawkins, Dawes, Posey, and countless others have held for their own purposes.

These families' existence and their refusal to let go of their identity history are threats to white supremacy in America. Perhaps if I had known their stories earlier, my childhood wouldn't have been marked with stammered responses to questions about my race.

I distinctly remember one of my well-meaning white high school teachers bastardizing Black history. It wasn't a class about Black history. We had just finished discussing a few Supreme Court cases. And with pity in his eyes he looked at me, the lone Black boy in the class, and said, "It's a bad world out there for you."

While yes, the world would be harder for me as a Black boy becoming a Black man, my teacher had reduced me and my history to a few highlights: a long period of slavery, some rights afforded to us that we couldn't quite discern. He left me with little to appreciate about my skin tone while extolling white folks who "gave" me rights. He had bought into the same reductionist view of history and identity and could only manage to shed his tear, look at me, and say, "It's going to be a bad world out there for you."

My teacher, white as he was, knew that he had benefited from this simple sorting: white and nonwhite. He knew that I had been dealt a bad hand. So I became the subject of his pity.

Remember: Native Americans, Creeks included, weren't a race until people like Henry Dawes made them into one, counting fictitious quanta of blood, telling Black Creeks that they were too Black to be Creek. As the Creeks bought into the notions of race and racism and anti-Indigeneity when Claude Cox orchestrated the changing of the Creek constitution in 1979, they effectively kicked out most of the Black Creeks, Cow Tom's descendants included. Excluding Black folks from an independent Nation that for generations had embraced them made the Nation just that much whiter. It was a feather in the cap of white supremacy. Blackness became the great simplifier, removing any remnant of the beautiful complexities of being part of the Creek Nation.

Today, we limit what opportunity those who are not white can have, what purchase on advancement they can enjoy. We tell kids of color, kids like me, to pull ourselves up by our bootstraps after centuries of fiddling with our access to our American identity.

The project of white settlers was to eradicate America's first people, the Indigenous, either through war or through civilizing them. Think back to what Dawes wanted to do to and for the Indigenous:

> When that time comes there can be no reservation to abolish or to perpetuate; no Indian agent to appoint or dismiss; no treaty to keep or abrogate.

This, however, was not the project for Black people. Use us to build an economy that supports white capitalism. Subjugate, leverage, deploy, and exploit us to generate capital. Define us legally as less than human as you empower white settlers and slavers to number us. Make sure the first law on the books in Oklahoma, the former Indian Territory, is a segregation law—an ode to Jim Crow. Tell the Blacks they can't be in the same train cars, bathrooms, schoolhouses, restaurants as the white folks. Tell them that Blacks can no longer marry their Creek brothers and sisters but tell the white folks that they can.

And what about the Simmons family? What do you do with

people who can boast of an ancestor, a Creek chief named Cow Tom, who negotiated deals on behalf of not only the Black folks but all Creeks? Dawes and countless other "helpful" white men throughout history had an answer: Make them Black. Make them Freedmen even when this family boasts never having had shackles around their ankles, hands, and necks. That's how you dilute your history. You let a someone else, someone white, dilute whatever power that Black Creek history and identity have given them.

The Simmons family, like the rest of the Black Creek families clamoring for their rights, produce tension, generated by a hierarchy that neither Black folks nor Creeks ever wanted or requested.

White supremacy in America has been trying to tell all Americans that race is biological. Trying to convince us that there's nothing wrong that trying to be as white as possible can't fix. White supremacy has been telling Americans that race-making is simple— a person is Black if any drop of Blackness can be found in them— while also telling us to forget that the single-drop rule of Blackness was just a way of counting more Blacks to use as free labor. Slave labor.

White supremacy has been telling me that I can't be complicated. That my Jamaican-ness somehow makes me less Black than anyone else, with less ability to claim every aspect of my lived Black experience in this country. White supremacy has been telling us through our laws, our curricula, our schools, and our capitalism who we ought to be in order to be as close to the expectations of whiteness as possible.

Cow Tom, Cow Tom's descendants, and those fighting in the courts today tell me: that ain't what that is. They and I are the expression of the journey to here, the journey to belong even when

America tells me that we don't belong. The identities of those on the margins are messy assemblages of joy and pain, triumph and tragedy, rising and descending hope in what this country could be.

So now, my origin explanation is told with more confidence than before. I am who I am because my ancestors were fully Black and fully Jamaican. I am fully American and carry with me every bit of the stories that made me. The stories of the Black Creek inspired my reexamination of who I am and where I come from. And so should such stories help us all. Despite the wishes of some, America can become a big table, with room enough for everyone with their strange, complex, beautiful past, present, and future. But only if we grab hold to the history that without telling in all of its difficult, ugly, yet hopeful ways could continue to divide us.

In writing this, I'm asking you not to give up on your vision of America. I'm asking you to make America even more beautiful—to actively paint a bigger picture, a richer one that encompasses all the things we've been, all the ways we've been, so that we might realize all we can become.

ACKNOWLEDGMENTS

There are many ways to describe the process of researching and writing this book. I could say difficult. I could call it herculean, but it was always possible because of the willingness of a longer list of people than I have available space to name. The reality is that this work stands on the shoulders of many others, both those living and those who have transitioned. That said, I must express my gratitude to a smaller circle of supporters who have enabled this story to find its way to these pages.

The fellowship of friends, other writers, and collaborators made this book possible. Chief among those people I am in fellowship with are the members of my family. To my wife, Dr. Ramone Williams, your unwavering support as I spent many days in parts of Oklahoma you had never heard of, time in libraries and archives and on calls with archivists who unlocked the veritable keys to the knowledge kingdom, will never be forgotten, and I love you. During the process of crafting the proposal and selling this book, discouragement came in spades, and your willingness to uphold me with prayer, love, affection, and affirmation got me through. To my parents and siblings, I thank you for understanding why after graduate school I'd spend so many days on your couches in Tulsa chasing down leads for stories that at times seemed they'd lead nowhere. But more than that, I appreciate that you cultivated my knack for writing even as a young child. To my mom, who gave me an F+ on a writing assignment when I was six years old, during additional homework after the actual homework had been completed, I thank you for acquainting me with the process of revision.

To the funders of fellowships such as the New America Fellowship, and the Shorenstein Center on Media, Politics and Public Policy, which greenlit and funded part of my time at *The Guardian*, where I first wrote the feature article that would lead to this book. Thank you to Jessica Reed, Oliver Conroy, Amana Fontanella-Khan, and the rest of the *Guardian* team. For my fellowship at Demos, I thank Sabeel Rahman, Arlene Corbin Lewis, Jennifer Fenton, and other colleagues who made room for me to spend long nights at the Demos offices placing pen to paper.

To experts in the field who routinely answered questions, lent their insight, and told me where to look for answers, you gave me, even in the burst of email responses, short calls, and more, the encouragement to continue writing. This book would not have been possible without a community of fellow writers with whom I found communities of commiseration. In particular, the Open City writing group that welcomed me, the nonfiction group at the Tin House Summer Workshop in 2019, and the mentors—Adam Serwer, Dr. Scott Ellsworth, Dr. Khalil Gibran Muhammad, Mitchell Jackson, Jackie Woodson, Kiese Laymon, and so many more—who told me that I could do this.

Perhaps most important, to the Simmons family, to the Black Creek families who entrusted me with their stories, and to Damario Solomon-Simmons, whom I could call a collaborator in the effort to help the world understand that these un(der)told stories matter: I cannot, without fighting an ever-flowing flood of tears, tell you thank you enough. I intruded on your lives and you opened your doors. You invited me into your homes, wrestled with me about how I would render the story of Black Creek identity and history. Damario, even your willingness to give me access to your grandmother Johnnie Mae before she passed and her willingness to take me on a journey through your personal history unlocked the scope of my literary and moral imagination. All of this willingness, all of this generosity, all of this consultation, trust, and free providing of the documents, artifacts, and mementos that ring your story and your family's story aloud, made this possible. And to the Black people who fight for their stories beyond the Simmons family, I thank you and promise you that I'll tell your stories. Because your stories might help our American identity find footing in a history we've often forgotten.

Last, I want to thank Kristin van Ogtrop, who took a chance on an MBA student who found more interest in telling stories than financial modeling. You helped get this book from ideation to selling, and I thank you for it. To my agents, Suzanne Gluck and Andrea Blatt, and the rest of the WME family, thank you for the continued advocacy on my behalf. And to Jake Morrissey, your sage advice, your expertise, and your guidance along this book-writing journey made my ideas sing, made the stories cohere, and brought to light an aspect of American history we desperately need to learn.

AUTHOR'S NOTE

Telling this story first required living in archives. The Oklahoma Historical Society, the Western History Collections at the University of Oklahoma, the Indian-Pioneer Papers oral history collection, and so many more sources brought me back home to do this work. The archivists, from near and, because of COVID, more often than not from far, guided me on my then-pedestrian navigation through an overwhelming tonnage of material.

Oddly, much of our histories, both lived and intellectual, can be found strewn across collections of now defunct newspapers. Many of these newspapers are held in the Chronicling America collection of the Library of Congress, an indispensable resource. Archivists who combed through records at the Department of the Interior, and the diligent work of the Descendants of Freedmen of the Five Civilized Tribes and the various organizations that have started to catalog the experiences and capture oral histories not taught in textbooks lit the way for me to see other aspects of history that were not available elsewhere.

There seems to be almost a canon of Freedman and Black Native

American literature that makes the entryway into the archive that much wider. Though I cannot name every single work used in preparing this book, I do want to highlight several that signaled paths otherwise hidden from view: the work of Dr. Tiya Miles; Angie Debo's foundational texts; Daniel Littlefield's critical studies at the Sequoyah National Research Center and his countless books and articles; Dr. Kendra Field's *Growing Up with the Country*; and Dr. Alaina Roberts's exploration of the struggles of the Chickasaw and Choctaw Freedmen. Dr. Claudio Saunt's work provided a road map for detailing the lives of those who have long passed but who left behind bread crumbs along the trail of their stories and legacies. Gary Zellar's work on the Estelusti provided a comprehensive, beat-by-beat rundown of what transpired decades before. While there are many more, these authors took up residence in my mind and haunted me every time I approached the task of writing these stories.

Because many of the more current activities of the Creek Nation and its aspiring Black members have landed in court, combing through legal documents became a critical way to tell the story. Contacting the Creek Nation's official leaders and getting them on the record was a path I found dimmed. Thus legal documentation became perhaps one of the most illuminating ways to access the information necessary to illustrate this story for you, the reader.

Finally, this story would not be possible without the hours of oral history that have been recorded. I wish that my education had emphasized the importance of oral history—capturing it, analyzing it, and disseminating it. The stories of Black people whose families found home in the Five Nations—Rhonda Grayson, Eli Grayson, Damario Solomon-Simmons, Johnnie Mae Austin, Sharon Lenzy-Scott, Dr. Alaina Roberts, and so many more—animated a history that I otherwise would have never known.

INDEX